Th[e]
Crui[ser]

Des Sleightholme was born in 1920 and started sailing at the age of 15. He has skippered almost every kind of craft from Yorkshire coble to gaff schooner.

For twenty years he has been a full-time yachting writer, and for the last nine years editor of *Yachting Monthly*, a leading journal for cruising sailors. He has written four books on sailing. His particular interest now lies in the family sailing cruiser and he owns a modern 24ft sloop.

Earlier, Des Sleightholme sailed for a living by delivering yachts, became an Outward Bound instructor, then a charter skipper and founder of the Island Cruising Club. Eight seasons of off-shore racing on the staff of a yachting magazine did nothing to shake his love of cruising. He has been wrecked, run down by steamer, dismasted and involved in fires at sea; he just happened "to be in the wrong boat, in the wrong place, at the wrong time...". Des Sleightholme is married and lives on the east coast of England.

Peter A. G. Milne is now established as one of the leading illustrators of small boats in books and magazines. A practical sailor himself, he lives in sight of the water at Christchurch, Hampshire.

J.D. Sleightholme

Illustrated by
Peter A.G. Milne

Fontana/Collins

Photo – Peter Johnson

This is Cruising

First Published in Great Britain by Nautical Books,
an imprint of Macmillan London Ltd 1976

First issued in Fontana Paperbacks 1982
Second impression January 1984

Copyright © United Nautical Publishers S.A. 1976

Text set by BAS Printers Limited, Over Wallop, Hampshire
Printed in Italy

Also available in Fontana
THIS IS SAILING by Richard Creagh-Osborne
THIS IS WINDSURFING by Reinhart Winkler
THIS IS FREESTYLE WINDSURFING by Peter van Wagensveld

CONDITIONS OF SALE
This book is sold subject to the condition that it shall not, by way of trade or otherwise, be lent, re-sold, hired out or otherwise circulated without the publisher's prior consent in any form of binding or cover other than that in which it is published and without a similar condition including this condition being imposed on the subsequent purchaser

Contents

Know your boat 8
Drifting behaviour 10
Letting go of the helm 11
Hull and sail balance 14
Reducing weather helm 16
Reducing lee helm 17
Stiffness 18
Windage 20
Windward ability 22
Auxiliary power 23
The effects of heeling and pitching 24
Propeller side effect 25
Handling under power (calm) 26
Handling under power (fresh breeze) 27
Tight turning (wind abeam) 28
Tight turns (wind ahead or astern) 29
Going alongside 30
Berthing in marinas 31
Marinas 32
Leaving a berth 34
Berthing stern-to 35
Stopping by going astern 36
Engines can fail 37
Preparing for sailing 38
Sheets 40
Cleats 41
Luffs 42
Sheeting 43
Working on deck in safety 44
Safe sail handling 46
Stowing sails 48
Cockpit drill 50
Getting the feel of her 52
Carrying her way 54
Slowing and stopping 56
Confined waters – Handling in wind and current 58
Anchors and anchoring 60
Room to swing 62
Letting go the anchor 64

Letting go on a reach 66
Letting go/Wind against current 67
Weighing anchor 68
Picking up a mooring 69
Shortening sail 70
Reefing gear 71
Improved reefing methods 72
Sail shape 73
Changing a headsail 74
Man overboard – Gear and what to do 76
Recovery 78
Knowing ropes 80
Securing with synthetics 82
Coiling 83
Halyards 84
Heaving a line 85
Crewing 86
Watches 87
Crew strength considerations 88
Planning a cruise 90
Passage making preparations 92
Accurate instruments 93
The weather 94
Planning the legs 95
Tidal strategy 96
Final approach 98
Harbour lights 99
Errors in pilotage 100
Drift and leeway 101
Helmsman's error 102
Log errors 103
Anticipation 104
Horizon errors 105
False headlands 106
Angles can deceive 107
False headings again 108
False fixes 110
False soundings 111
Deceptive chart scale 112

Deceptive buoyage 113
Coasting complications – Apparent wind 114
Wind bend 115
Coasting complications – Headlands 116
Thermal wind 117
Coasting complications – Fishing craft 118
Seeking shelter 120
The coastal passage – Temporary anchorage 122
Coasting complications – Haze 124
Current inset 125
Fog 126
Fog – The radar reflector 128
Positioning the reflector 130
Fog tactics 132
Entering harbour 134
Prepare your yacht 135
Bad weather 136
Bad weather dangers 138
Making for shelter 139
Land and sea 140
Flooding 142
Cockpit 143
Action 144
Emergency equipment 146
Rescue 148
Helicopter rescue 149
Yachts and shipping 150
The open sea 152
At night 154
The tender 156
Dinghy Handling 158
River bars and shallows 160
Calculating depth 162
Eating and sleeping 164
Sleeping at sea 166
Index 168

The Cruising Sailboat

When *This is Sailing*, the first colour book from United Nautical Publishers, passed the quarter million mark of sales in nine languages, it was less of a compliment to the book, than to the phenomenon of yachting as an international sport.

By using colour on every page—drawn by Peter Milne under the direction of Richard Creagh-Osborne—it dug into the practicalities and the feeling of sailing in a way that had unarguably never before been attained on paper. *This is Sailing* used a modern lightweight centreboarder to teach how to sail expertly, but not everyone has this type of boat. All over the world sailors are moving up to—or starting from scratch in—cruisers. These are not cruisers of the old school with baggywrinkle and meat safes, but usually glass fibre, invariably Bermudian sloop rigged, probably under 30 ft or 10 metres and with berths for a family of four or five.

This is the boat which you are going to learn to sail and handle well in the following pages. By sailboat cruising is meant being confident and skilled in moving on the water with family or friends, in light winds and strong, in good visibility and bad, by day and by night. Nor does cruising always imply voyaging or even passage making: here the concern is to handle the cruiser properly whether leaving a marina berth for a few minutes to get some fuel or preparing for a three-week cruise to a foreign shore.

The colour graphics have two major advantages. First, the techniques recommended in the diagrams are vivid: indeed the pictures will speak to you direct, with the words sometimes only there as assistance. Second, it has been possible to reproduce closely cruising situations: for there are few photographs of cruising at sea. If your experience is limited, you can be assured that before long you will come across the very scene that has been described here.

Section by section

The mechanics of sailing have been discussed in *This is Sailing*, but on board a cruising sailboat free to drift on the water you are on a wholly different platform from an open unballasted centreboarder in the same circumstances. *This is Cruising* begins from this point.

Des Sleightholme's colour picture scheme drawn by Peter Milne, then considers the cruiser's qualities and what they imply when moving along the water under sail and power—hull and sail balance, stiffness, windage, pitching, propeller effects, turning in breeze and calm. One really can take one's boat out—book in hand—and try these experiments.

On page 30 you begin to meet objects other than water, hard objects like quaysides and marina berths. So the author goes on to deal with 'Stopping' and how to keep away from danger. Only then can preparations for sailing begin and discussion of the most effective drills in various manoeuvres.

Longer passages are implied around page 86, where crew considerations emerge, then passage planning, navigational and weather preparation and tidal strategy.

What do you see when you make your landfall? The answers to this question cover those pages which some will find the most valuable part of the book. Des Sleightholme has uniquely developed over the years the art of graphically representing 'navigation by eye'. Here the technique is illustrated in colour which has not before been possible. The unpleasant but anticipated situations of fog, bad weather and even rescue from a yacht are in the closing pages.

And afterwards

Sailing and especially cruising, breaks down international barriers and this book has already done so as well. Because as you read it, sailing men overseas are looking at exactly the same visual presentations, though the words are in eight other languages—and being used in more than eight other countries, particularly the English, French and Spanish versions. Even after the words have been read, the diagrams and cruising scenes, aided by either imagination or hindsight, can be used again to envisage variations on fresh aspects of sailboat cruising.

UNITED NAUTICAL PUBLISHERS

Know your boat

To the sailor there is just sheer pleasure in being afloat on the water. This pleasure can be savoured best in the ballasted cruising yacht. In such a boat on a mooring, even in a marina berth, the boat pulls and moves according to wind and current: this constant movement, or potentiality for movement is probably a major contribution to the 'on board' feeling.

But knowledge of the boat begins with learning to harness the pull and movement to make the yacht do what is required. Sails, engine, rudder, keel, the action of wind on hull and structure all play their part, whether the skipper wants it or not. Sails can be lowered or engine switched off but the others always have to be taken into account. Before trying to go places, it becomes worthwhile to analyse the boat's behaviour to sea and wind regardless of sails and engine. Sometimes when the wind on the mast blows her head off, one wishes that the mast was not there at all, but it is and has to be remembered and its effect anticipated.

Hauled ashore on dry land (or dried out after running aground!) is the only time the boat is motionless. A boat never ceases to move, even when moored. Unmoored, she drifts with the current **A** or drifts with the wind **B**, she swings, bobs, rolls and pitches, or she is given forward motion so that she can be steered, or motion astern steering with the rudder reversed.

According to her hull shape, windage, rig and her manoeuvrability – her size or her type – she will be easier or harder to handle under power or sail. Learning the characteristics of one's own boat is the first step in learning to handle her smartly.

(1) She may have a long keel or a fin-and-skeg, a small mainsail with a short foot plus a large headsail, or she may have the opposite. (2) Her hull may have a canoe, a counter or a transom stern – a variety of rudders. (3) She may be of light displacement and low wetted surface with a fin ballast keel or her hull may be 'all boat' with a long keel and considerable wetted surface area. (4) Likewise her shape and area on the waterline may vary from (a) full with little overhang at bow and stern to (b) fine, (c) powerful and buoyant aft or (d) beamy but fine at bow and stern. In every case not only will the handling characteristics be different but they will change according to the force of the wind and the heeling of the hull.

Drifting behaviour

If allowed to drift with rudder free, a sailing cruiser tends to 'seek the wind' with her stern **A**, but her attitude may vary from almost beam-on to stern to wind. She may wallow straight down wind or she may make a certain amount of headway.

It may be possible to steer her down wind under bare spars **B** and retain good control or there may be very little control. Knowing what can be done may someday get you out of a tricky situation.

With the rudder free to swing she may just lie solidly beam-on or she may 'hunt' around, **C**, drifting slowly or even quite rapidly to leeward according to hull shape and windage. Long keeled hulls **D** tend to drift more consistently than short keeled craft, but not invariably so – you must find out. You must also find out how she will lie if the tiller is lashed amidships or to leeward. All this knowledge of the boat will soon become applicable.

Letting go of the helm

Under sail, a boat has different characteristics. If we let go of the tiller when lying closehauled **E** she may continue to sail herself, luffing or bearing away a little in the wind puffs or **F** she may simply luff herself head to wind, tack herself and lie hove-to with jib a'back. She may even display lee helm characteristics and do the complete opposite, bearing away as in **G** instead of luffing and perhaps even gybing.

According to wind strength and the sails carried, each boat will vary in character and behaviour. From light breeze to strong, storm jib to big genoa, an owner will discover new differences in balance and he will learn to anticipate them.

Letting go of the helm

If the helm is released when reaching with the mainsail well freed **A** she may luff and lie with sails a'shake or tack herself and lie with jib a'back. Or if under a very large genoa she could pay off downwind instead. When running wing and wing (main and headsail on opposite sides) **C**, she would probably behave as in **B** (left) – but she might also gybe.

Under headsail or mainsail only her behaviour **D** will alter completely, as it would under deep reefed main and working jib. It is important to know by how much it will alter.

(Right) Two cases of understanding behaviour in an emergency. In **E** the engine has stopped (1). A jib is set, she is luffed and she lies, jib a'back, helm a'lee, safely stemming the current to permit quick repairs (2). At **F** a single crew gets his anchor up in bad weather. He knows the rate and direction of drift to be expected and time available for lashing and stowing it.

E

1   2

F

13

Hull and sail balance

When heeled a boat will not be as simple to handle as when cruising upright.

(Left) **A**. Sails apply forward pressure to a mast but when heeled it passes outside the hull centreline **B** and tends to turn the boat into the wind. In **C** we have drive (y), side pressure (w) and side drift (a). In **D** drift is resisted by water pressure. (b)

E. Imagine a plate pushed at its exact centre of lateral resistance – or similarly a hull profile **F**. If we find the exact centre of effort for the sails (COE) and contrive a rig in which it comes just ahead of the hull centre of lateral resistance, it will balance out the luffing tendency. In **G** (w) is the COE and (b) is the CLR.

H. This is how the design might appear with COE (a) and CLR (b). **J**. As the hull (a) heels, the shape of the waterline immersed changes, (b) thus a short beamy hull presents a less symmetrical shape than a long, fine keel.

K is typical of the imbalance when sailing a small cruiser with weather helm. She is trying to push up to windward and continuous pull on the tiller is necessary by the helmsman.

Reducing weather helm

On the wind some boats carry considerable weather helm, needing the helm constantly held to windward. **A**. Raking the mast forward (1), shortening the boom (2) and extending the fore triangle (3) help to reduce it by moving the COE further ahead of the CLR.

Sail setting also helps. **B**. A boom vang flattens the sail, allowing the boom to go further outboard – no drive lost due to sail twist. **C**. Dotted line shows boom amidships when closehauled, creating weather helm. A sheet traveller allows proper trim without boom lifting. Early reefing of mainsail before changing down from genoa and allowing the mainsail (**D** to **F**) to 'feather' while sailing on a genoa all help to correct weather helm tendency.

Reducing lee helm

Some boats which even carry moderate weather helm in stiffer winds, tend to turn down wind in light winds, needing the helm pushed to leeward (lee helm) to compensate.

Bad lee helm can be reduced by **G** raking the mast aft and reducing the size of the headsail, sometimes (**H**) deliberate heeling by the crew assists and **J** trimming slightly by the bow also helps.

Stiffness

A. Sailing with the rail under (left) may feel exhilarating, but the boat is slowed. Sails do not harness the wind efficiently (compare with right), leeway is pronounced, and steering is difficult with the rudder heeled to an extreme. Some boats are not as stiff – that is, they heel more readily – than others. Adequate beam and a ballast keel produce a sail-carrying hull. A beamy hull needs less ballast to make her 'stiff' but she must be sailed fairly upright or her immersed hull shape becomes asymmetrical.

B. A boat's righting moment – her ability to resist heeling forces – is largely a function of buoyancy and gravity. Boats (a), (b), and (c) are examples of design underwater. When heeled (b) and (c), being beamier, will have more heeled buoyancy than (a). Boats (1) and (2) have the same 40 per cent ballast ratio (percentage of keel ballast to total weight). Though (1)'s ballast is carried lower than (2)'s, their stiffness, or sail-carrying ability, will be about equal due to (2)'s beaminess.

C. Stiffness is also increased by means of waterline length. The waterline (x) is lengthened to heeled waterline (y) by immersion of bow and stern overhangs. With less overhang, (w) does not gain as much additional buoyancy.

For speed, racing boat designers aim for minimum wetted surface, or underwater area (1), at some sacrifice to stiffness and interior roominess. Cruisers (2), needing more sailing comfort and accommodation, yet desiring a degree of swiftness, are apt to be a compromise.

Windage

When, in a very small cruiser, accommodation requirements, headroom etc are rated as more important than sailing efficiency, the result is **A**, a short, dumpy hull with high windage and excessive beam which is poor to windward.

Cruiser **B** also has four berths but she is a bit larger than **A** with less windage for her length, a finer hull shape and better stability or stiffness. She is the frequent compromise between comfort and performance.

Boat **C** on the other hand, is a cruiser/racer but with performance rating highest. She has little headroom for her length, great stability and a much finer hull form. Her bulb fin keel and her overhangs give her speed and high windward performance.

Let's look at these three boats in a fresh breeze. Small, dumpy boat **A** is steeply heeled, losing effective sail area and creating great hull windage, making poor windward going.

Boat **B**, suitably reefed, makes good progress without crew hardship. Boat **C**, not yet reefed, is going fast to windward but her crew needs to be tough and dedicated to stand the discomfort for very long.

There is a limit to the amount of windward-going punishment – flying spray and violent motion – that a family cruiser crew can take before they are forced to slow down. A high performance crew in a high performance boat can keep beating to windward long after a weaker crew has been forced by exhaustion to give up. Conversely, no crew however expert, can beat to windward in bad weather if the boat is ill designed. The compromise of sail power allied to sea-kindliness and crew comfort is the aim of all good cruiser designers.

Windward ability

Could you beat off a lee shore in a gale? Boat **A** certainly could not. Under sail alone her excessive leeway and lack of sail power turn her close-hauled course into a broad reach. Use of engine also might make only slight improvement.

B Few small cruisers are wrecked in this way though. Wind direction is seldom constant for long and *any* shift makes one tack a better offshore one than the other. Cruiser (a) cannot weather the headland but a wind shift (thick arrows) used to advantage (b) allows her to point further offshore and weather the headland.

The experienced skipper is constantly alert for wind shifts and wastes no time in using them, knowing well enough that the wind may shift back yet again. He also knows how and when to combine engine with sail power.

Auxiliary power

Both boats **C** and **D** have 40hp engines but whereas the planing boat **C** uses most of her power, heavy hull **D** wastes much of it in propeller slip or cavitation. She needs a slower turning, larger and more coarsely pitched propeller to give 'bite'.

Boat **E**, a sailing racer, only needs a small power unit for harbour work but boat **F**, of heavy displacement, needs solid thrust for head wind slogging – a more powerful engine with 3-blade propeller slow-turning for a coarse bite.

Motors themselves, like cruisers, are a compromise. Propeller drag, while sailing, spoils performance but propeller power for motor-sailing demands a propeller which is of correct size and design for maximum efficiency. Without this, a propeller may produce maximum boat speed in a calm sea **G** but lack drive, due to cavitation, in a head sea **H**.

The effects of heeling and pitching

The usefulness of an engine to assist windward sailing in rough weather is limited if the propeller is close to the surface. At **A** it is well immersed when the boat is upright and it is operating in dense water. When she is well heeled in a strong breeze **B**, the propeller is brought closer to the surface. It is thus working in water of lesser density and at times it will be exposed altogether as the boat pitches.

When the yacht is also heeling and pitching, typical of motoring in a head sea (**C** and **D**), engine efficiency may be cut by 50 per cent. If the propeller itself is smaller than it should be – chosen for its low drag in interests of sail performance – efficiency will be even lower. A propeller must match its engine and work in dense water.

Propeller side effect

Water density increases rapidly with depth. The blades of a spinning propeller, biting denser water in the bottom half of their circle than in the upper half, exert a side-paddle effect.

Imagine a box with a wheel at one end **E**. If the wheel is turned as shown, the end of the box will move to the right. A righthanded or clockwise turning propeller tends to kick the stern of the boat to the right as well as driving forward **F** – to a lesser extent of course. Slow-turning large diameter propellers have pronounced side effect.

G. With a stern bias towards starboard the boat tends to turn her bows to port when going ahead. With engine astern though (propeller turning left handed) the reverse happens – stern to port, bows swinging to starboard. The pivot point red dot moves aft when going astern. Note the rudder banging itself hard over due to water pressure when making sternway. (Green arrows, bottom right.)

Handling under power (calm)

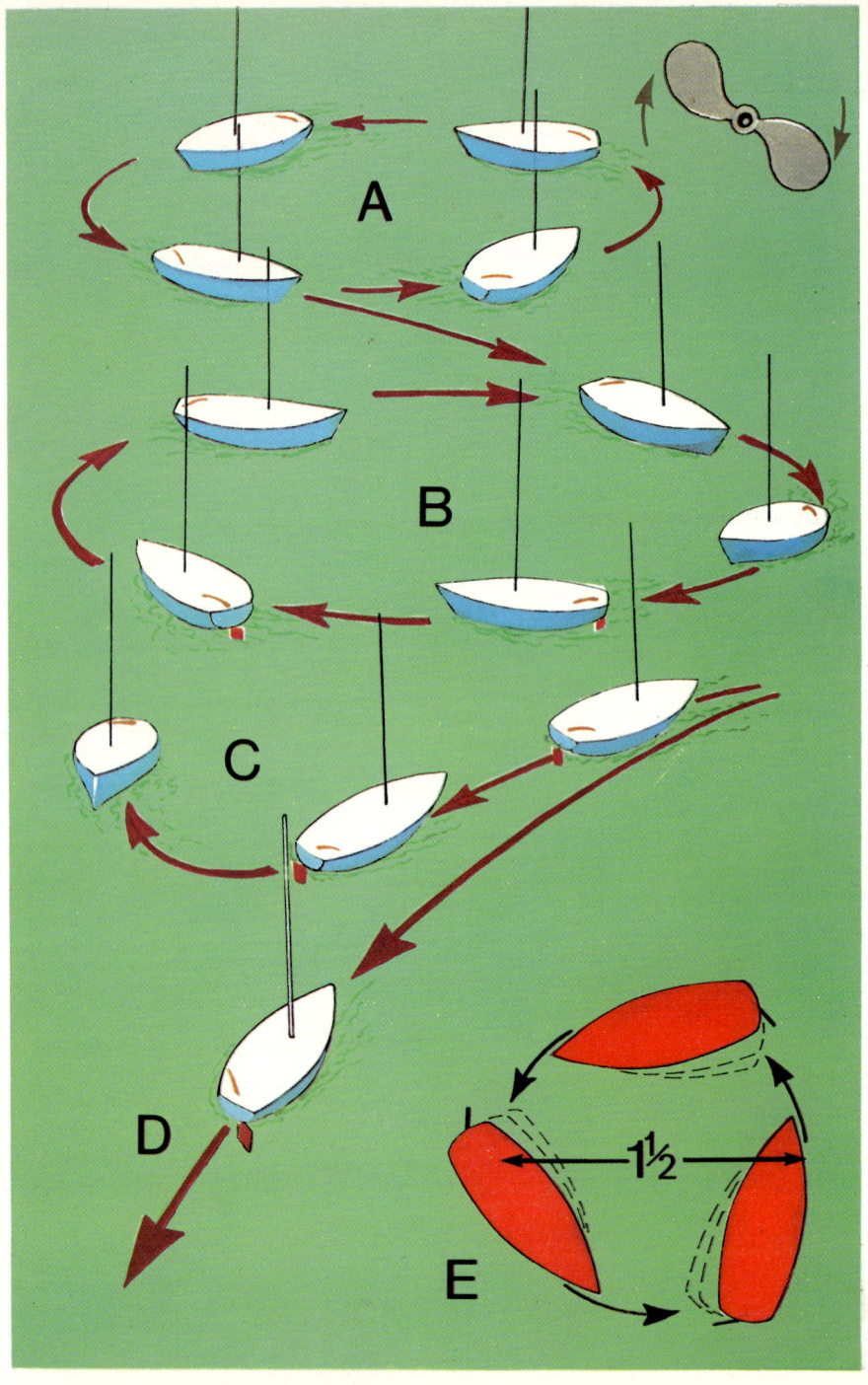

Propeller side effect can be used in manoeuvring. With a righthanded propeller a circle to port will be tighter than one to starboard (the opposite with a lefthanded propeller) **A-B** shows the effect of a righthand propeller of considerable side-kick. In reverse she will turn her stern to port **C** but she may not turn it to starboard **D**. (Opposite effect for left handed propeller).

Auxiliaries can seldom be turned tightly by alternately going ahead and astern and relying upon helm assistance, but short, hard bursts ahead on full helm, alternated with short, hard bursts astern (no helm change) to check headway often work. The modern auxiliary cruiser will however usually turn in about $1\frac{1}{2}$ lengths, engine ahead on full helm, **E**. Note how the stern swings outwards.

Handling under power (fresh breeze)

Without sails or engine, no headway, a boat will always swing her stern to windward, bows downwind (1-2-3). This 'wind-seeking' or weathercock tendency is at the root of all power handling in a fresh breeze.

In **F1** to **F4** the cruiser with the wind abeam can be turned *downwind* easily and tightly because her stern wants to seek the wind. In **G1** to **G4** an attempt to turn her bows into the wind is more difficult because it is contrary to the wind-seeking rule. If, additionally, she has pronounced propeller side-kick to starboard (in this case), a turn into wind to starboard might prove impossible.

Some craft, due to windage and side-kick, can only be turned one way into the wind. Many need full helm and full engine to turn them into wind.

Tight turning
(wind abeam)

Not all cruisers will turn in just over a length; it also needs confidence to attempt a full-ahead turn in a confined space. The blue yacht is making an ahead-astern turn. At 1, 2, 3 she goes ahead turning upwind and then goes astern (4, 5) using her stern-kick to port (right-handed propeller), finally going ahead again (5, 6).

The red cruiser uses a different tactic, she goes ahead (1–2) and then makes a stern board (3) utilizing both her astern kick to port and the wind-seeking tendency to take her well up wind (4–5). She then goes full ahead on full starboard rudder (6, 7).

Much depends upon room available, whether there is also a current to allow for and the individual performance of the boat. In an emergency don't just go full ahead and hope and don't rely upon the stopping power of the engine astern.

Tight turns (wind ahead or astern)

The blue cruiser (1, 2, 3) turns to starboard because her right handed propeller will then give her stern its kick to port as she goes astern. This starts her stern wind-seeking, (4), she then goes ahead again, (4–5). The red cruiser with the wind astern has a more difficult turn to make. She hugs the river bank in order to have maximum room for a turn to port – her tightest turn with a right-handed propeller. She then turns on full helm, (2, 3, 4, 5) with plenty of power, but her helmsman must gauge whether she'll make it before she fouls the anchored purple yacht.

In a strong wind some cruisers might not be able to get round into the wind. No other manoeuvre would work either. All that can be done is to set the mainsail and sheet it hard for a second attempt. If this fails she must anchor, swing and then up anchor and proceed. If there is a current flowing *against* the wind even this is dubious.

29

Going alongside

A. Assuming a kick of stern to port with engine astern, an approach (1–4) head to wind, allows a slow approach with stern slewing towards the wall as the engine is given a burst astern. If circumstances dictated a *starboard* side to wall berthing, the stern kick would be a hindrance and the engine would be used to slow her more gradually.

B. Current ahead, wind astern. She must stem the current, going astern to slow and slew her stern in. Rapid work with mooring lines is needed, if wind and current are together, berth heading into both.

C. With wind abeam as shown, beware bows falling to leeward as she slows and loses steerage way. In the final approach steer off the wall a shade, letting her blow in bodily.

Berthing in marinas

D. In a strong cross wind and making for a berth, boats **E1** and **E2** will need very different handling, due to their different turning ability and power handling characteristics. You must know your boat.

Some craft will be sufficiently manoeuvrable to be taken straight in but others may get out of control as soon as steerage way drops and their bows will pay off downwind. If the manoeuvre is plainly not working out as planned, it is usually safer to go hard astern out of the berth and make a second attempt. The temptation is to begin an attempt to manoeuvre by going ahead and astern in rapid succession. In such conditions it seldom succeeds.

Marinas

Long keeled boat **A** has played safe, berthing on the end of the finger pier (1–2), securing at (a) for a few moments until stern line is also secured. She is then allowed to drop back, her crew controlling her on her lines (b) until she is berthed (3). Given a big engine and a fast crew she *might* have been taken straight in and stopped astern, if the crew were smartly ashore with lines. The price of error is daunting.

Modern boat **B** is highly manoeuvrable and *might* have been run straight in, stopped dead on engine and secured. Such craft are often very easily handled astern and an approach (1–2–3) is practicable, sheering across wind with stern a little upwind. If making for the leeward berth approaching stern to wind (**C**) is also possible.

In all cases, crew work with lines can make or mar any manoeuvre. Train your crew.

Leaving a berth

A cruiser in berth **A** has a simple task. She will drift clear of the berth as soon as lines are let go. She can then motor straight out.

Cruiser **B** is held against the pontoon pier by the wind. Her bows must be pushed clear before she can be motored out. She must go straight ahead though because any attempt to steer to starboard will swing her stern into the pier. Crew uses a boathook to bear off.

Had she been berthed bows-in, she could have been motored out astern – again using the astern kick to port and wind-seeking tendency to take her clear.

Make a habit of thinking out every manoeuvre before letting go. Note wind and current, also the movement of other craft. Tell your crew exactly what you are about to attempt.

Berthing stern-to

The procedure of anchoring, then manoeuvring stern-first into a berth. **C** With wind abeam, an attempt is foiled by stern swinging upwind. Crew handle her in alongside the already moored yacht. Cruiser **D** has a man detailed to check the out-running anchor cable in order to 'twitch' her bows straight. Cruiser **E**, with good astern control, motors astern straight in.

In strong beam winds, motoring in bows first to secure a long line to the quay, then motoring out stern first will allow the boat to swing up stern to wind. She can then go ahead, lay her anchor and back in under control between anchor cable and stern line.

Remember, in a strong beam wind, the anchors of yachts already moored will be to windward of their berths. Place yours also a little to windward of the vacant berth.

Stopping by going astern

Only practice makes it possible to judge stopping power by going astern. Going full astern as at **A** can cause the stern to swing out of line on the approach, (1–2–3–4), necessitating a burst ahead to correct it. A gradual application of reverse gear, retaining helm control, is usually better. With wind astern she will be sailing in under bare mast.

B With fore knowledge of good astern power when needed though, an approach in neutral, sailing on the mast, then simultaneously going hard astern and securing a stern line (**B** 3–4) may be possible. Faulty crew work could be a hazard. A propeller in reverse gives far less power than it does in forward gear. It may stop her on a calm day but have little effect in a smart following breeze.

Engines can fail

Making allowance for the unexpected is good seamanship. Given a choice, never motor close to windward of a danger like this yacht near the shore with sails stowed – in case the engine fails.

Boat **C** plays safe but **D** hugs a lee shore. Boat **C1** passes the safe leeward side of a moored craft rather than shaving by to windward. Heading into a strong current boats do not risk a close turn round the bows of an anchored craft but play safe, like **C2**, and give it a wide berth upstream.

Preparing for sailing

Whether a cruiser goes to sea for a half hour sail or for an extended passage, she must be fully operational and ready to stand up to any emergency. This means that she must be competently crewed and that she must have her full equipment aboard, including charts, navigational instruments and the gear needed for sailing at night.

It is easy to argue that with a quiet day sail in view and the sails, rigging and engine all in good condition, there is no need to equip her with distress signals, food, water, bedding all the essentials for prolonged cruising. Many an owner, out for a short sail, has found himself the victim of circumstance – perhaps on account of a sudden offshore blow combined with a failure of gear – and had to fight his way home in an ill-prepared boat. In a small boat you either go to sea or you stay in harbour and going to sea means going prepared for what the sea can do.

Prior to any sail, no matter how short, an owner should have up-to-date weather information and he should continue to listen to radio forecasts as he goes along. He must also study local conditions and watch his barometer because official forecasts are not always either recent or accurate in local detail.

There must be drinking water in the tanks and a full tank and reserve supply of engine fuel, also warm clothing and oilskins, lifejackets and bedding for all crew.

For the same reasons, boat and engine maintenance should be an on-going practice. The little breakages and weaknesses that accumulate can combine to cause a major fault usually at the worst time and it is unwise to leave them until 'a suitable opportunity' to cope with them occurs. Keep a maintenance log book.

1. Look at the spreaders in case some other boat has been alongside in your absence and caused damage aloft – it could mean the loss of the mast.
2. Check navigation lights and battery regularly.
3. See that anchor and cable are always ready for use.
4. Make sure that rigging screws are properly locked and/or seized.
5. That the bilge pump is in working order.
6. Fuel and reserve tanks full.
7. Lifelines not worn or damaged.
8. Engine properly serviced and easy to start.
9. Warps and heaving lines ready for use.
10. Lifebuoy ready for instant use complete with light.
11. Distress signals up to date and in easy reach.
12. Steering compass corrected.

Sheets

The sheets are the hardest worked lines aboard. They must be supple but strong, thick enough to grip but not too thick or they will not render easily in light airs. Plaited dacron is ideal.

Headsail sheets should be long enough to permit the sail to be freed right off when running. Short sheets inhibit control of the boat, but if they are *too* long they create a hazardous tangle in the cockpit. A mainsheet must run easily through its blocks and be long enough to square the boom fully off when running.

Headsail fairleads must have generous range for adjustment and be easy to alter **A**. Try setting a storm jib to see if it can be sheeted correctly. It may be necessary to have special fairleads fitted, **B**. Check that the mainsheet slider **C** moves easily and that the limiting stops **D** can be adjusted readily.

Cleats

A jamming cleat **E** offers rapid, easy and quick release but it can be tripped accidentally in the dark. There is a limited range of rope thickness that can be used in a particular size of cleat.

A mainsheet which is rove as shown, with the lower block incorporating a cam cleat **F** is an excellent idea and a boon to the single-handed owner. The sheet can be instantly released – it can however also be tripped free accidentally by someone standing on the fall of the sheet.

A cleat with pointed horns **G** can be a danger to crew and the design serves no useful purpose. The broad horned cleat **H** is safer and the additional area provides extra frictional surface. It is better to have any cleat a shade too large than too small.

Luffs

Sails are designed to be hauled out firmly along the luff and the foot in order to put shape into the sail. A mainsail luff may need a tack tackle **A**, if halyard winches are not fitted or in the absence of some other means of tensioning it. The kicking strap (or boom vang) **B** holds the boom down and reduces mainsail twist.

Headsail luffs can be tensioned by means of a halyard winch **C** or/and a tack tackle **D**. The fall of this tackle may be led aft to the cockpit for easier adjustment.

The luff tensions of main and headsail are varied according to wind strength, being set up hard in fresh breezes and eased away in light airs in order to put more shape into the sail. They are never allowed to become completely slack though. A headsail with a scalloped luff is a sign of a badly run boat.

Sheeting

Mainsail and headsail must be individually set and trimmed but they must also be regarded as working together as one unit. Correctly trimmed, the airflow over, round and between the sails is smooth and unrestricted. The 'slot' between headsail and mainsail must be kept open and even in order to achieve maximum rig efficiency.

E. Reaching with sails trimmed too flat. Loss of drive and harmful turbulence at back of mainsail.
F. Mainsail sheeted too free and backwinded by air flow from the headsail.
G and **H**. Sails properly trimmed together and the slot working efficiently.
J1. Sheet lead too short resulting in a slack foot and a taut leach.
J2. Sheet lead correctly in line with the sail mitre (middle) seam. Even tensions on foot and leach.
J3. Sheet lead too far aft resulting in a tight foot and a slack leach.

Working on deck in safety

Constant alertness, good balance and secure footing plus instinctive use of grab points are essential. **A** Grab points at: pulpit, harness hook-on wire, shrouds, guard rail, after pulpit, grabrail, forestay, backstay.

Danger areas **B** where crew is at risk due to being off balance are marked in red. Foredeck, out of reach of mast, rails or forestay; hatch top; cockpit/sidedeck climbing area; after deck.

C shows safest areas (green) where there is adequate grab hold and protection. Beware complacency though. In bad weather more people have gone overboard from the cockpit than from the foredeck.

D. A man on the foredeck may be out of grab reach and a harness won't stop him from going overboard. Fixed grab points when going forward or aft should be used, but a (red) line rigged from mast to deck cleat provides extra hold. Unwary stepping on wet synthetic sails **E** which are very slippery is dangerous and it is safer to kneel or sit **F** in rough weather. The wise man always hooks an arm around any convenient stay when both hands are needed **G**.

Safe sail handling

Wind-filled sails represent power which must be controlled by sheet and halyard. Slipping wind sheds power but the flogging sail creates noise and violent movement. Freed from the control of sheets and halyards, sails can balloon and take charge if wind is allowed to fill them. Always stay to windward of a flogging sail, muzzle it quickly or spill the wind out of it, then lash it securely.

A. Shackles used to attach sheets to headsails can cause injury when the sail is flogging. **C**. When lowering a headsail be sure to secure the fall (the end) so that it cannot run aloft, also hitch the head of the sail to the pulpit by its halyard to prevent it riding back up the stay – or better still remove halyard and snap to becket on pulpit – and lash the sail to the pulpit with a tye until there is time to unhank it. It is safer to attach sheets to sail by making short-up bowlines **B** instead of using shackles or patent clips.

Violent motion in a seaway makes the stowing of a mainsail dangerous. Before a man is allowed to begin stowing the lowered sail be sure to secure the mainsheet properly, hitching the sheet around the block as shown if it is a cam-block type. Failure to do this means a risk of the boom swinging out over the side carrying a crewman with it. In such conditions safety harness should always be worn.

Never stand upright on the coachroof – kneel or sit. See that the head of the sail is hitched by its halyard to a cleat on the mast so that it cannot balloon up the mast track, torn free by the whipping of the halyard.

The worst conditions for handling and stowing sails are when the wind is astern and there is a rough following sea because the motion will be a wild, rolling lurch and the sails, being attached by their luffs to mast or stay, will be most prone to ballooning. If possible try to come head to wind and lie quietly while sails are being stowed, reefed or changed.

Stowing sails

A headsail can be stowed in its bag **A** while remaining hanked to the stay. Sheets must be disconnected and the halyard either secured or unclipped and snapped on to the pulpit. Bag stowage keeps a sail clean when handling warps or anchor and leaves it ready for instant use. A very temporary stow **B** requires the halyard to be well secured otherwise its jerking will tear the sail free.

Stages in stowing a mainsail. **C** Pull the leach forward to form a bag into which the loose bunt of the sail is bundled. **D** Pull out a fold from the foot and shake the loose sail down, then roll up on to the top of the boom. **E**. Pass sail tiers or gaskets criss-cross and tie.

Cockpit drill

TACKING. A cruising helmsman tacks at a speed to suit his crew, slowly enough for them to sheet home before the sail fills and makes unnecessary winch work for them. (1) 'Ready about'. Crew casts off sheet from cleat. (2) 'Lee O'. Helm down and crew spins sheet turns off winch. (3) Crew homes the new lee sheet, takes a couple of winch turns and spins in all slack, takes more turns and begins winching. (4) Final sheet trim and secure.

GYBING. The aim is to gybe without swerving wildly off course. If the mainsheet needs hauling in and paying out (heavy weather) the helmsman may nudge the tiller over with his body, leaving both hands free. In light airs and an all-standing gybe he sees that the slack sheet does not foul as it passes over the stern.

(5) 'Gybe O'. In mainsheet and helm over. (6) Boom across. Helmsman puts helm up to correct swing, pays out sheet. Crew handles headsail. (7) Steady on course. (8) Little swing off course has been accomplished.

51

Getting the feel of her

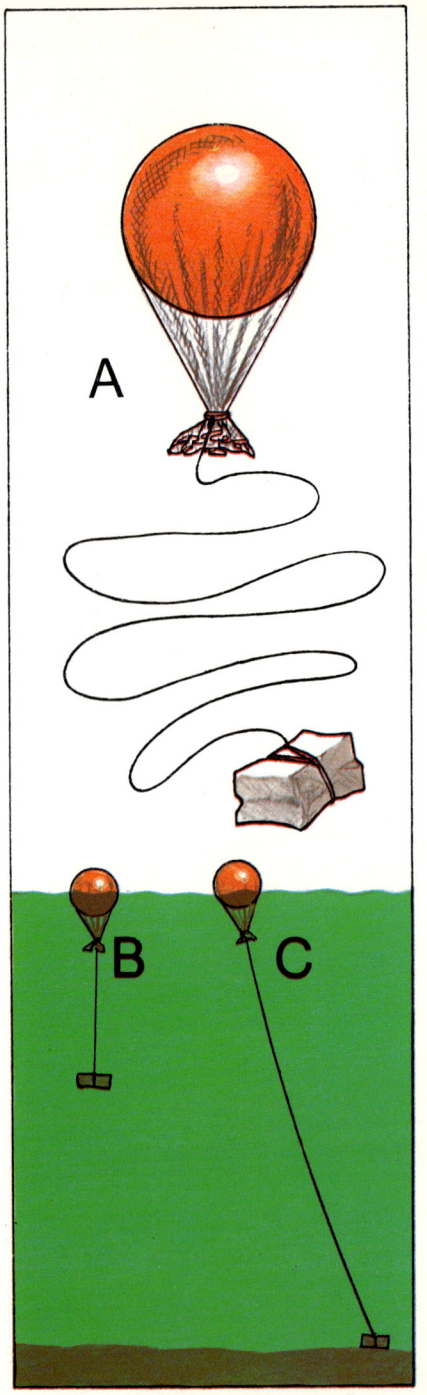

Sailing a boat around in circles and performing handling aquabatics will reveal what a boat can be made to do under sail and enable her owner to judge her capabilities. Don't always be content with a straight out and straight home afternoon sail: find a patch of clear water and learn about your boat. It may some day stand you in good stead.

A marker buoy made up by putting a toy beach ball into a net bag and hanging a heavy stone underneath it on a short line, **A** provides a manoeuvring point. Free-drifting buoy and boat will not be influenced by current, relative to each other, **B** but if manoeuvres in current conditions are preferred, the heavy stone should be attached by a line long enough to reach the seabed. The buoy will then be moored **C** and the boat will be subject to the current.

Try figure-of-eight turns using two of these buoys, first free drifting and then with the buoys moored. Try also stopping the boat between them, luffing to pick them up and any other manoeuvres you can think of. Encourage your crew to try also – he or she just might be left in charge some day.

Carrying her way

Wind and sea conditions constantly affect the amount of way a boat will carry. At **A** when sails are lowered, she continues to carry her way far down wind, 'sailing' under her bare mast. At **B** however luffing head to wind, the windage of hull and rig bring her to a standstill in perhaps one and a half lengths.

At **C** on a reach, the slackening of the sails by easing sheets slow her at first but as speed drops and the apparent wind comes broader on the beam, lost steerage way causes the bows to pay off and the sails to fill again. **D**. Only luffing will really slow her, or putting helm hard down and freeing the headsail completely.

Luffing head to wind in a light breeze **E** may allow way to be carried for several lengths and permit the mooring buoy to be picked up, but the same luff made in strong wind and rough sea stops her dead **F** and she pays off, out of control.

A luffing turn to pick up a mooring **G** also results in a dead stop. The full rudder and rapid change of direction robs her of forward way even before she comes head to wind.

Learning to judge how far a boat will carry her way is very difficult, but it is vital to know, whether under sail or engine.

Slowing and stopping

An owner needs to be able to slow down or stop his boat while under sail, to allow time for proper chartwork, for reefing or sail changing, or even to have a meal in comfort. A headsail can be let fly to spill wind completely on any point of sailing, but a mainsail can only be freed off until the boom touches the shrouds **A**. By heading a little into the wind though **B** and by lashing the tiller a'lee both sails can be 'feathered'.

Lying thus with wind abeam **C** the gradual loss of headway brings the apparent wind from forward of the beam further and further aft until the mainsail begins driving again (far left). Thereafter she may drift slowly ahead, luffing herself and paying off by turns.

Heaving to with headsail a'back, mainsail sheeted in and tiller lashed a'lee does not always work well in fin keeled craft, which may 'hunt' or swerve around **D**. However, with sails trimmed as in **E1** or **E2** the boat should lie quietly. All boats differ and one must experiment.

Heaving-to for lunch in a moderate breeze and doing so as a safety measure in bad weather are very different manoeuvres. In the latter case, mainsail only **F1** or small headsail only **F2** with tiller lashed a'lee may be the only practicable recourse. Rate of drift may be around 2 knots at right angles to the wind – much more in bad weather, but boats vary considerably.

Confined waters – Handling in wind and current

A. Tacking up a channel with nil or only slight current. (1) A cruiser tacks to gain an unobstructed next leg rather than follow dotted line. (2) Luffs a little to avoid stern moorings. Holds on as far as possible thus being able to clear the stern of the anchored vessel on the next tack.

B. Current against wind. (1) Luffs to carry between moored craft, tacks and bears off to crab across current keeping out of dead-wind area to leeward of vessel. (2) Hangs on current to get clear and tacks to avoid bows of moored craft. (3) Tacks rather than stand on between narrows.

C. (1) Can shave close down current of anchored vessel as she will be heeling away from it and now cable will be slack. Tacks short rather than work between anchored craft and (2), luffs well clear of and around the pier end. (3) and (4), short tacks to avoid dead-wind area to leeward of wharfs and vessels.

D. Here the current and wind are together. (1) Tacks in bare time to avoid losing wind under pier. (2) Luffs round pier head and continues as in **C**.

Anchors and anchoring

Anchors in small sailing cruisers should really be a shade heavier than the weight recommended for the size of boat. No anchor can be *too* big, or line *too* long when anchored, but handling the gear on deck can often be a problem. A smaller anchor may hold safely in an ideal seabed but it will soon drag if the ground is soft or if it is too hard for it to penetrate properly, even though it might be quicker to get over the side.

The deeper it can bury the better. A concrete block may at best exert a holding power of its own weight × 1–2 unless deeply buried or exerting suction. A conventional 'fisherman' anchor holds up to 7–10 times its weight on a sandy seabed, but plough and burying type anchors exert a hold of at least their weight × 30 – provided they are able to bury.

In normal weather a cruiser may only exert a few pounds of load but windage, waves, jerking and sheering in bad weather can double and treble the load.

The scope of line paid out is popularly quoted as being a requirement of depth of water × 3 for a chain cable and depth × 5 for rope, but this is an absolute minimum for normal weather only – unless a much heavier anchor is used. A rope line is improved by a short length of chain next to the anchor to assist a horizontal lead. There must be sufficient length of cable aboard to provide a scope of up to × 10, in really bad conditions – possibly even more in bad holding ground. Spare warps of suitable size can be added to the anchor line to increase the scope.

Greater scope will reduce jerking and snubbing but it may also increase the tendency for the cruiser to sheer about. It is the weight of a chain that provides its shock absorbence and the elasticity of nylon warp produces a similar effect. Without this the line may part or the jerks may break out the anchor.

A suitable anchor and a generous scope of cable is a form of insurance.

Room to swing

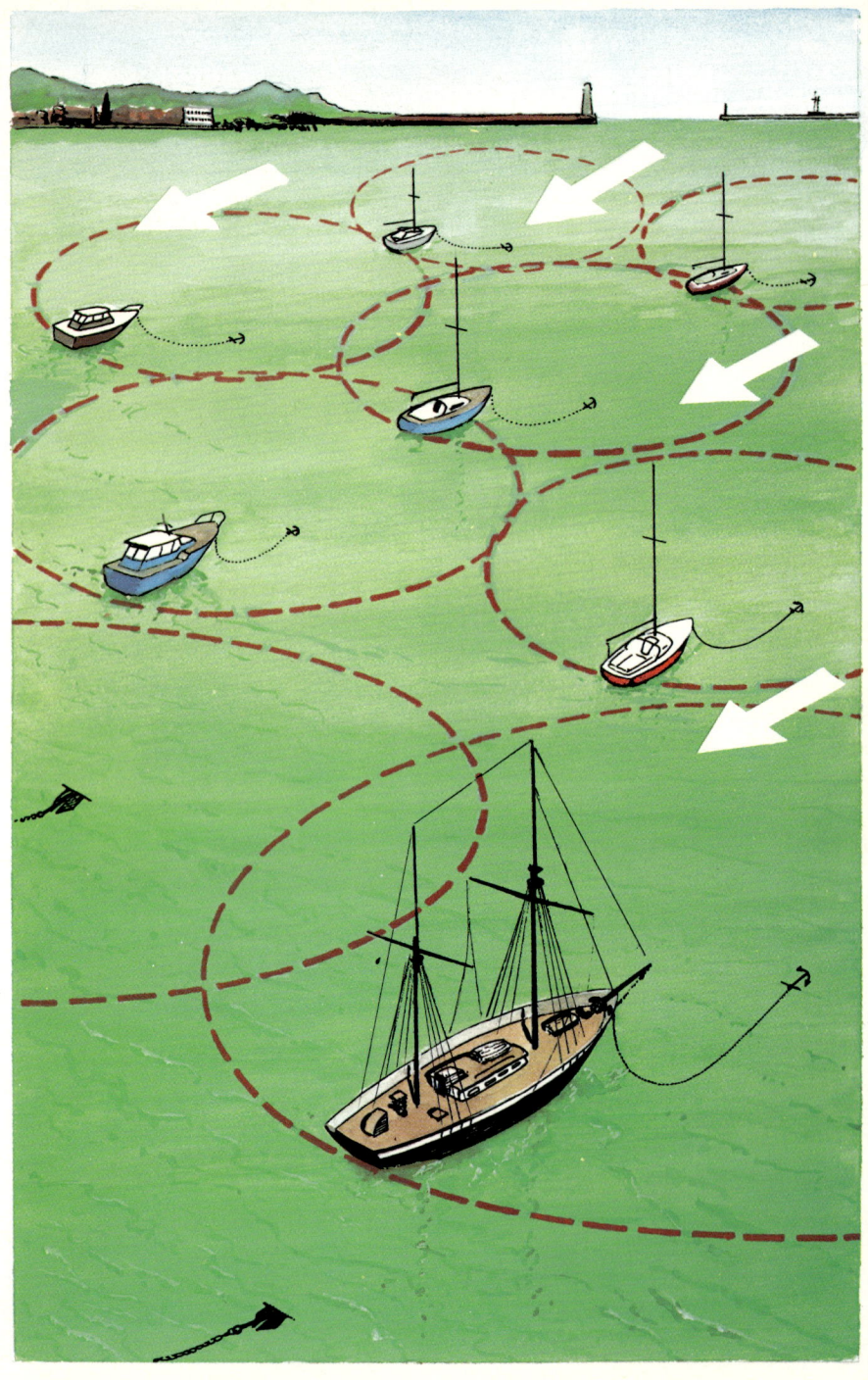

Every vessel at anchor or on a swinging mooring must have a clear arc of swing. The arcs of a number of craft moored or anchored close together may intersect, but provided all craft swing together and to the same extent and in the same direction they will not collide.

They may collide if some are of very different types to their neighbours. A boat with a long, deep keel lies more to the current than to the wind in lighter breezes but a shallow, light hull may do quite the opposite. Mast and hull windage are a big influence and some craft may 'sail' around their anchors when wind and current oppose, while others may simply take a sheer to one side and thereafter lie quietly.

At **A** all are lying to the wind, well separated, but at **B**, with current against wind, they have sheered in various directions, leaving open spaces between them. If a newcomer anchored in these spaces, he would find himself foul of his neighbours when the wind or current changed direction or altered in force.

In order to anchor correctly in crowded waters it is important to try to estimate where the anchors or moorings of nearby craft are positioned, relative to the actual positions of the boats using them.

Letting go the anchor

Having decided where the cruiser is to be brought up and therefore where her anchor must be placed in order that she will lie in the position chosen for her, the helmsman must manoeuvre his *bows* to the exact spot for letting go. If the boat is moving too fast, the anchor will not hit the seabed at the spot chosen, neither will it do so if the crew is slow in letting go.

Delay in letting go and/or paying out the cable ruins many good attempts **A**. The anchor should be slung outside the stem and the cable ready overhauled (hauled out of its locker and run back again to free it of kinks). A rope should be 'flaked' (see the sketch) and not coiled if it is to run freely.

B. The cruiser, (1), first circles the anchorage, her skipper sizing up the situation. At (2) he has selected his berth and he takes a sweep in order to be able to round up into the wind for letting go, (3). Time spent in conning an anchorage is never wasted.

C. Be prepared for the bows paying off downwind after letting go. The cruiser luffing (1–2) and letting go, will immediately pay off and begin to sail again (3–4). The crew must pay out cable generously or the anchor may be dislodged. Do not snub the anchor until it has scope enough to take an initial hold in the seabed.

Letting go on a reach

In a narrow channel the cruiser skipper should try to approach his chosen anchorage along the lee side of the channel, easing his sheets in order to slow down. If he carries too much way when he luffs up to let go, his way will make it difficult to judge exactly where his anchor will come to rest. At (1) she has luffed and having let go, (2), she overshoots her anchor, falling back over it, (3) and (4), finally bringing up head to wind at (5). It is important that scope is paid out smartly. It is possible that in falling back over her anchor the chain may disturb it and the boat illustrated has guarded against this by sheering to port with the last of her steerage way, to carry her anchor line clear.

Letting go/Wind against current

A running approach to the anchorage is made, reducing sail to the stage when she may even be sailing over the opposing current under her bare mast. In lighter winds, an approach under headsail only may be the right area of sail. At (1) the cruiser is under headsail, but at (2), to reduce speed still further, she has stowed this also and proceeds under bare pole.

She lets go anchor at (3) and carries her way past it, bringing up at the end of her paid out scope, (4), and then paying off beam to wind, (5) and (6). At this point there may be very little strain on her anchor, the cruiser being held between the forces of current acting on her hull and windage acting upon her rig. According to strengths of wind and current she may then either lie quietly, albeit beam on, or she may begin to sheer about at the end of her cable.

Weighing anchor

After breaking out the anchor from its hold on the seabed, it may be important to ensure that the cruiser pays off on a particular tack: perhaps only one tack leads clear into safe water. In **A**, at (1), she has her mainsail set and the headsail ready to hoist. At (2), when the cable has been shortened up almost to the point of breaking out the anchor, the headsail is set and backed so that as the anchor breaks out, it will force the boat's head in the desired direction, (3).

B. With wind against current the mainsail cannot be set until she has her anchor clear, otherwise, held by her bow, she will commence sailing around on her anchor. The anchor can be broken out, (1–2) and she can be run off downwind under jib until there is sea room to round up and set the mainsail.

Picking up a mooring

C. With wind against current the correct procedure is to lower the mainsail and approach against the current with wind astern. According to its strength the approach may be made under headsail or under bare mast. Never attempt the pickup under mainsail. The moment the bows are secured to the mooring, the boat will sheer wildly and she may gybe violently.

D. When a current does not have to be allowed for, a broad reaching approach to the buoy is easiest, perhaps under mainsail only to leave the foredeck clear. The mainsail has been freed off to slow her. It is hauled in a little in order to give her more steerage way and it is spilled again near the buoy to slow for the pickup.

With wind and current both together, a closehauled approach and a final short luff to the buoy is the only safe method.

Shortening sail

A. Reefing while still sailing fast to windward is quite pointless when cruising. Slow her by easing sheets or by lying with helm a'lee and headsail eased, or, if making a headsail change, lie with the mainsail eased well off. The saying, 'the time to reef is when you first think about it' is a wise one and a reef put in early is usually a better reef than one done under stress. Reefing early when strong wind is imminent may leave the cruiser temporarily under canvased – the engine can be used to maintain speed, pending the arrival of the wind.

The smaller the area of sail carried, the more vital it is to ensure that the sails are well set. In bad weather resistance of hull and rigging increases so sails need maximum efficiency for windward work.

Reefing gear

B. Points reefing, used properly, results in a well setting sail. **C**. A variation of it is a laced reef or a system using elastic cord and a row of hooks along the boom. In both cases, pennants at tack and clew take the main loads and these are hauled down and secured first.

D. Roller reefing is simpler to use in the dark but does not guarantee a well setting sail. The gear may have a worm drive and handle (have a spare on board) or it may be of through-mast design, which is both simple and efficient. A drawback of roller reefing is that it makes the use of a kicking strap (vang) difficult.

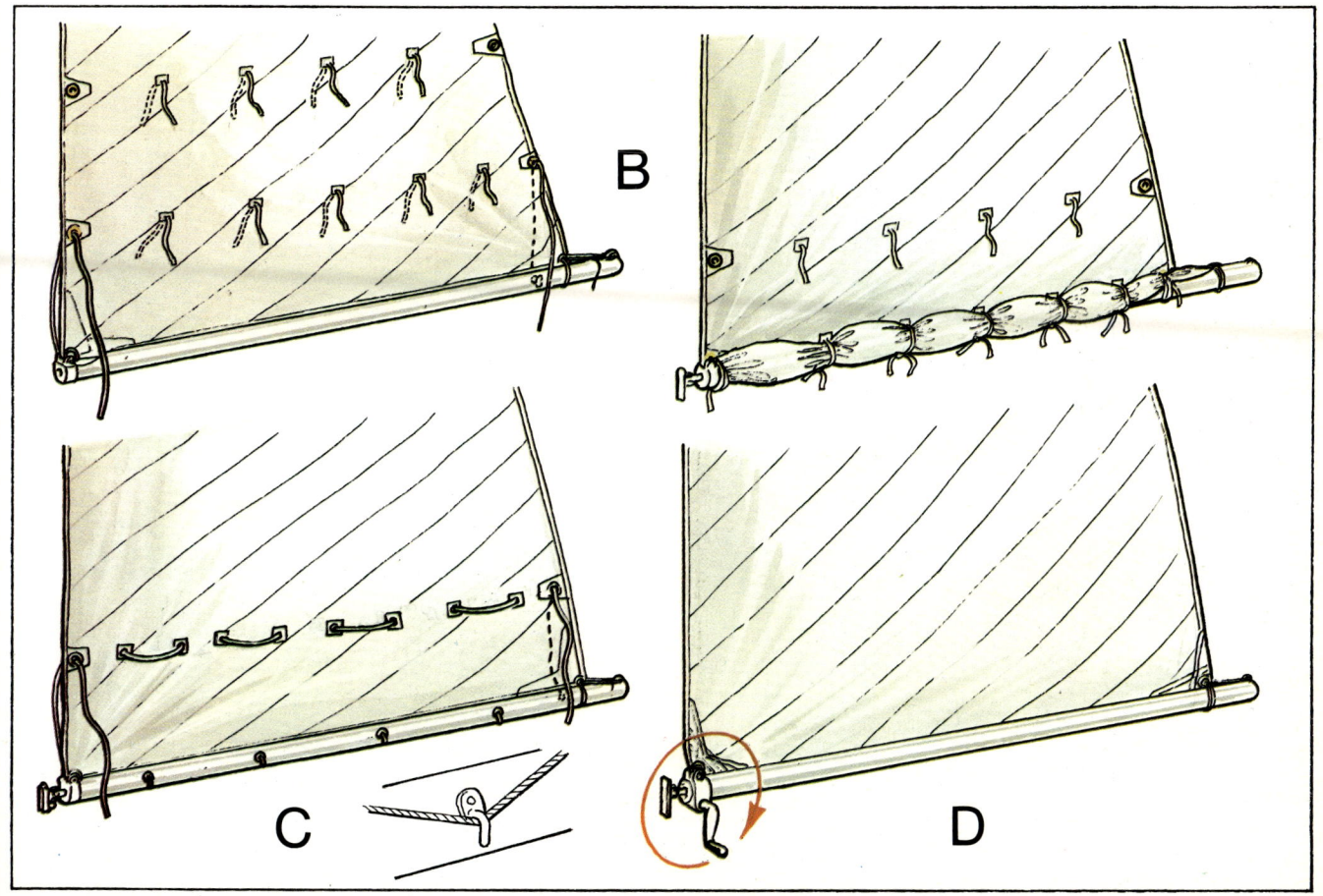

Improved reefing methods

A. Jiffy reefing has found favour over older methods. Cringle in luff is pulled down to one of the hooks at the tack and leach cringle is tightened down by means of small block and tackle or winch on the boom. Even in small yachts some form of purchase must be used. Loose sail can be laced up or just bundled loosely for short periods.

B. To alleviate poor sail setting in roller reefing try inserting battens as the sail is rolled down to tauten set.

Sail shape when reefed

C and **D** contrast the result of effective reefing and one which is badly organized. In **D** loose luff to jib and boom menacing cockpit mean less performance just when needed in tight situations. **C**, with reefed sails well set, is reassuring.

Changing a headsail

The first move in shortening sail is usually the change down to a smaller headsail. As this frequently means that sea conditions have become rougher, the more forethought and system used, the easier and faster the job will be carried out. At **A1** the new sail in its bag is on deck and safely hitched to the cleat. (2), Sail lowered remembering to secure the halyard end to the mast. (3), Halyard unclipped and clipped to pulpit. (4), Sheets released from clew.

B5. Old sail bundled below and (6), new sail hanked on, beginning with the tack but remembering, (7), to hitch its empty bag to a cleat to avoid loss.

C. Sail bag safely below, (8), and, (9–10), sheets and halyard attached, back to the mast and hoist.

D. It is sometimes better to hank on the new sail below the bottom hank of the existing sail. This means that the period during which the cruiser is sailing without a headsail set is much shorter. While this is usually of importance only when racing, there are times when a cruiser headsail change must also be carried out quickly and without losing sail power. The change then consists of lowering the existing sail, unhanking it quickly to clear stay and, after changing halyard, hoisting new sail. At least one (leeward) sheet must be on new sail. Subsequently old sail is removed from stay and stowed.

Man overboard
– Gear and what to do

Coping with this emergency may call for great skill, self control and presence of mind. The more thought and planning given to it the greater the certainty of success. First considerations are the victim's ability to swim or to stay afloat – hence the importance of always wearing a lifejacket – and to keeping an eye constantly fixed upon the person in the water. Throw one lifebuoy immediately and then sail back close to him with a second lifebuoy available. Now there is time to think.

The boat must be stopped dead, right alongside him, which means that an approach must be made from downwind of him. At **A**, a gybe if made *at once* might bring the boat back to him head to wind. At **B**, under spinnaker, a reach off at 90 degrees gives time to hand the spinnaker and to return on a reciprocal heading and at **C**, a simple reaching return following a gybe to get downwind permits full control of speed. There are no classic manoeuvres which will guarantee success, only forethought and calmness can do that – *doing the right thing under existing circumstances*.

The temptation may be to lower all sail and start the engine and in some cases this may be right. A spinning propeller is a terrible danger to a man in the water though and once the man is alongside and secure, the engine must be *stopped*, not merely put into neutral, before attempting to haul him aboard anywhere near the after end of the boat.

(1) Lifebuoy with a drogue or a 'skirt' to prevent it from drifting in the wind and out of reach.
(2) Self-operating light float attached to lifebuoy (also a whistle).
(3) Dan buoy flag marker.
(4) Floating throwing ring and line.
(5) Heaving line.
(6) Boarding ladder.

Recovery

There are three major risks: losing sight of the man; delay and its consequences for a poor swimmer, especially in cold water; difficulty in hauling him back aboard. The latter can be a monstrous problem. The combined efforts of the man in the water and his rescuer(s) grow less with each unsuccessful attempt to pull him up and final exhaustion may overcome all — with fatal results. Panic exacts further toll of stamina. First, he must be reached and kept afloat.

At **A** a buoy has been thrown hastily and it is out of the man's reach. At **B** the cruiser is put about and passes close enough for a second buoy to be put into the man's hands. At **C**, she returns, under full control on a reach and with a boarding ladder ready in position. **D**. Lifelines should never be shackled to the after pulpit – a lashing can be cut, leaving a clear space for working. With a pair of wires only the lower need be cut. A rope bight or loop can be rigged with one end around a sheet winch. An active man can climb aboard on this, but not a weakened person – he should be secured with a bowline around the chest pending aid aboard.

A proper boarding ladder is the best aid of all but lacking one, a weakened swimmer can be pulled into a half-inflated dinghy **E**. (It can be carried permanently on deck in this state) from which hauling aboard is easy. Another method is to turn the man face outboard and lift with one man at each shoulder.

F. A method which has been known to work in real trouble, when the person is both heavy and weakened, is to drop the boom end into the cockpit and sheet it fast. The mainsail is then run completely out of its mast track and bundled overboard. By dragging the person into its slack and taking up on the halyard with each roll of the ship, he can be hauled up to deck level.

79

Knowing ropes

Use the right rope for the job and choose the best. Modern synthetics are hardwearing, long lasting – the better quality being treated to withstand sunlight, which can be injurious. Different types of rope are designed for various uses. **A**. 3-strand nylon has elasticity and is used for anchor lines and warps. Dacron/Terylene has rather less elasticity. **B** is plaited with a straight laid core, a pliable rope for sheets. **C**. Double plait is softer and used for dinghy sheets. **D**. Cheaper synthetics can be used as floating rope, for mooring lines and rough uses. With these ropes knots tend to loosen themselves and are sometimes liable to parting if strained over a concentrated area. **E**, pre-stretched Dacron used for halyards where elasticity is undesirable.

Basic knots, hitches and bends. **F**. Reef knot for joining ropes of similar thickness. **G**. Figure-of-eight knot for stopper knots in ends of sheets. **H**. Clove hitch – a securing hitch. **J**. Rolling hitch used to secure to a rail, cable or stay when the pull is parallel and constant in direction. **K**. Fisherman's bend for securing to an anchor or similar purposes. **L**. The bowline, a non-slip bight.

All these knots, bends and hitches are prone to come undone when made in certain types of synthetic Always leave plenty of spare ends and haul properly tight. It is important to be able to make these knots at top speed, also in the dark and to make them in ropes and lines of any thickness. Knowing which to use when is a matter of practice. For instance, with heavy warps of equal thickness it would be safer to use two interlocking bowlines to join them rather than a reef knot. The knots shown here are a small selection of the many in regular use and every effort to learn the other common ones should be made.

Securing with synthetics

A. An end tucked back through the lay will guard against this bowline coming undone. **B**. A seizing of small stuff on the ends is even more secure and it does not fractionally weaken the rope as it does in tucking through the lay, which disturbs the rope construction. **C**. This bowline on a post might lift itself off if the rope was stiff and springy, a complete round turn as shown makes it more secure. **D**. The tugboat hitch, used when securing to a post, for example when making up an anchor warp or chain, never pulls itself so tight that it cannot be undone easily, as in the case of certain other hitches. The bight of the slack end is taken under, up and over as shown several times. It cannot come undone.

Coiling

E. Most ropes are laid (twisted) right-handed or clockwise and they must be coiled clockwise. The coils are laid from one hand to the other, shaking out any twists before each coil is handed. The exception is certain double plaited ropes which are not coiled but allowed to form natural figure of eight loops.

F. A buntline hitch is the correct way to make up a coil so that it can be used later. Pass the bight over the head of the coil.

G. Stopping a coiled warp is essential if it is to be readily usable in a hurry. Use yarns pulled from odd short lengths of rope or else use breaking stuff, easily snapped.

Halyards

Never make a halyard fast with only a couple of figure of eight turns or it will pull tight and may jam. **A**. Use a full round turn followed by two or more figure of eight turns. **B**. Jam the slack end hard down in the top of the cleat between halyard and cleat.

The coil can then be hung as shown in **C** and **D** by pulling a loop (bight) through the coil and settling it over the top horn of the cleat. If the bight is first taken behind (between standing halyard and mast) and then settled over the horn, it will be more secure.

Heaving a line

A large diameter coil cannot be *heaved* without risk of it fouling and a small coil carries further **E** and is easier to aim. Before throwing, divide the coil neatly and hold the main coil in one hand while heaving the remainder from the other.

F. This is how the line should run. The intention is to throw the coil high enough to carry its distance but no higher or it will expend its length in mid air. Practice throwing lines. When coming alongside it is vital to be able to get a line ashore smartly. Get your crew to practice too, initially trying the heave at an angle of 45 degrees.

Crewing

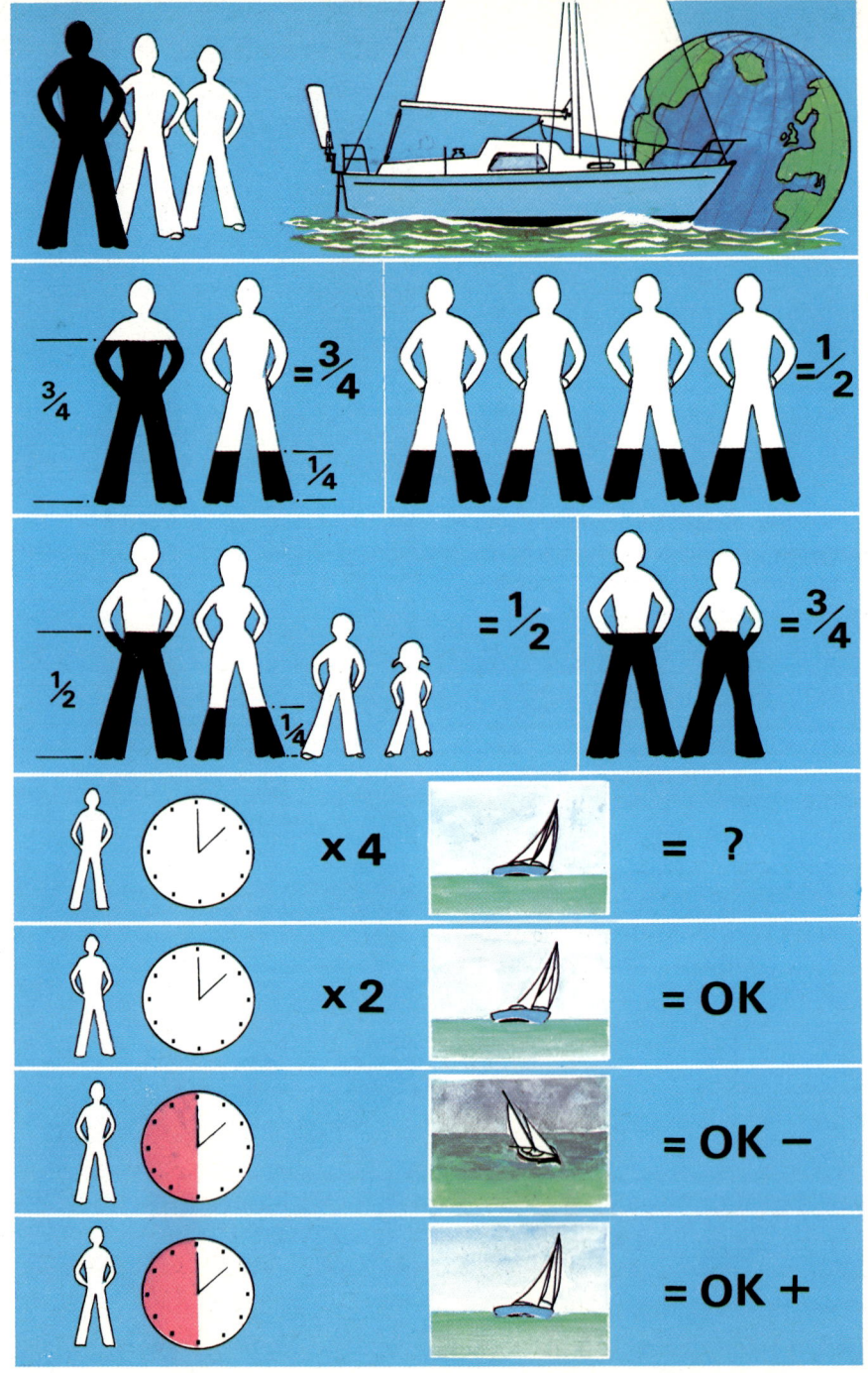

One fully experienced fit person can sail around the world non-stop, with or without extra crew. If we rate him as being 100 per cent efficient in terms of experience, it might seem that two crewmen of 75 per cent experience and 25 per cent experience respectively should be his equal in terms of crew power. Plainly this is not so. Neither would four men each of them 25 per cent experienced equal him. In practical terms the two men would perhaps total 75 per cent and the four men only half the experience of the lone 100 per cent man.

The diagrammatic sketches show how various family combinations might rate. The bottom sketches relate to staying awake ability based upon a fit man. Perhaps 48 hours in fine weather (but with impaired judgement), 24 hours safely in fine weather but maybe only 12 in bad, but under strain. A 12-hour watch in fine weather is no strain although tiring.

Watches

On a night passage crew alertness falls to a sharp low, usually after midnight, rising sharply with daylight. A three-man crew, consisting of fully experienced skipper and two half experienced people, might work night watches as follows:

- 20.00 – midnight (the two half experienced men)
- Midnight – 03.00 hrs (the skipper alone)
- 03.00 hrs Skipper wakes one of the crew
- 04.00 hrs Skipper wakes the other crew. Skipper goes off watch.

This type of system covers the low alertness period and ensures that the hand-over at 04.00 hrs is to a fully alert relief.

There are many variations of watch composition and duration. The best system is the one which fits the needs of a particular crew. The aim is to crew the ship at full alertness always.

Crew strength considerations

A vessel at sea is as good as her crew. In planning a cruise, the ability and the comfortable level of stamina demands upon crew are all-important.

A small 5–6 knot cruiser averaging *3 knots* may have a family aboard with father as the only (and 75 per cent skilled) working crew. In two weeks they might cover 100–200 sea miles. The chart shows the percentage of each 24 hour day spent sailing. The same boat with a crew of two experienced, fit men might cover 300–500 miles with ease.

The fast cruiser capable of 7–9 knots and an average *5 knots* could have a family consisting of 75 per cent experienced father, two 50 per cent experienced teenage boys and a less experienced mother. They made one 36- and one 24-hour passage in the two-week cruise, total mileage 400–600. The boys will not have the staying power for more. The two men and wives, all quite experienced, do more miles because they are a strong watchkeeping crew and can make more night passages.

The motorsailer, speed 6–7 knots, averages *4 knots* because the crew like sailing, could have a fairly experienced man and wife crew and cover 400–500 miles but watchkeeping is rather a strain for them on longer passages. An extra man aboard, and both men fully experienced, allow more night/day passages to be made in comfort and the 500–600 range is modest going.

These times and distances are based on normal weather, wind average Force 2–5. Bad weather and days spent in shelter could halve the above totals. In planning a cruise much depends upon the weather behaviour typical in the waters concerned. In some climates an itinerary is easy to follow, in others it is important to have very flexible plans, but in cruising it is the life afloat that matters and not the number of ports visited.

The needs of children and days in port for fun ashore must be allowed for. The needs of grown-ups too, who may experience an accumulating tiredness after a series of day/night passages, should be considered by the skipper.

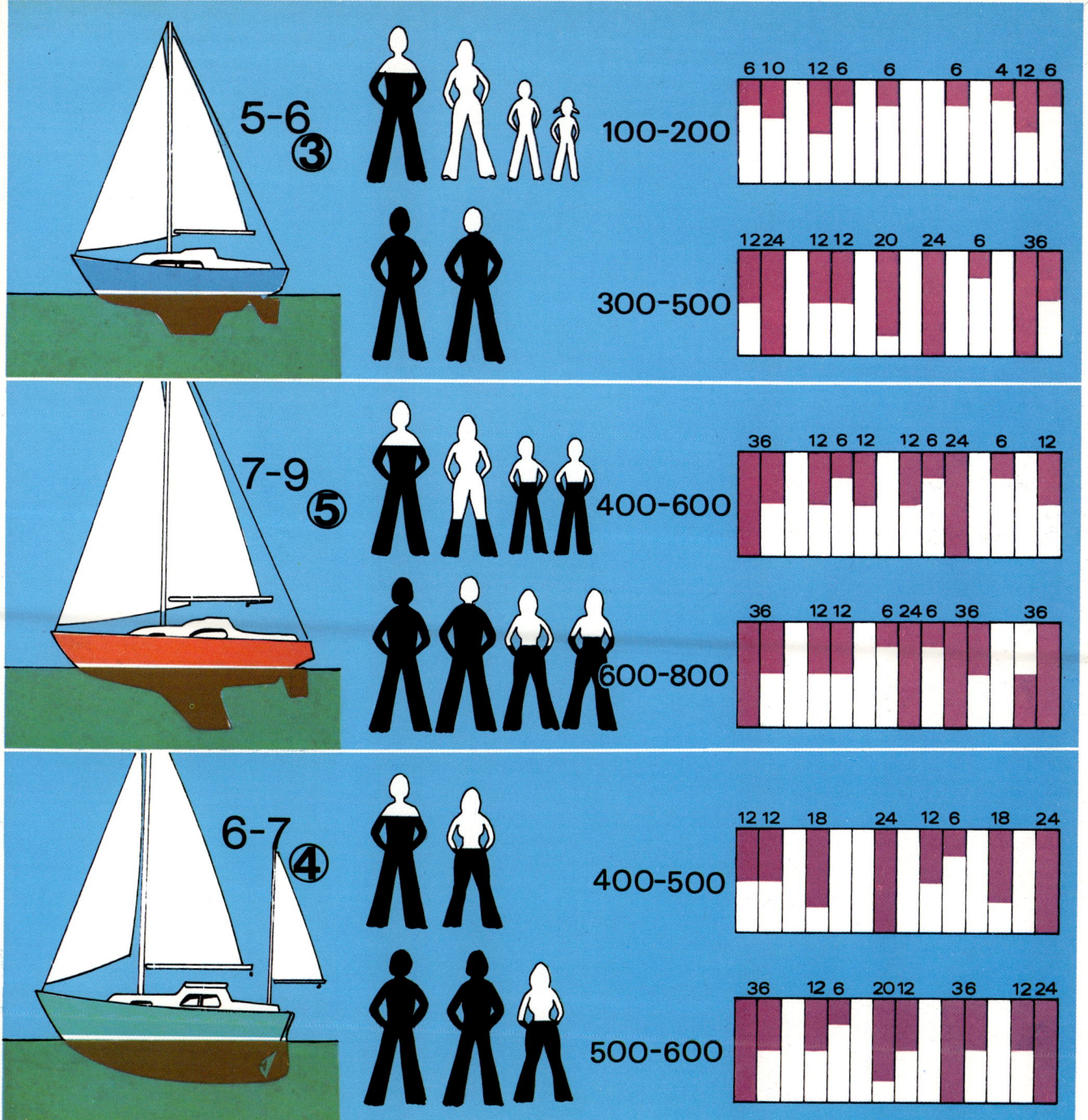

Planning a cruise

Pleasurable cruising under sail is not dependent upon distance covered in a given time. One must find the right 'pace' for each particular boat and crew. One can have more fun within a few miles of home than many have in covering vast distances.

How far – in how long?

The imaginary cruising ground shown here offers a choice of distances. Note the prevailing wind with length of arrow indicating likelihood of direction. Port **A** is a poor area with lee shores predominating. From it however two places can be visited on cruise, **A1** giving a round mileage of 520 with cruise **A2**, 560 nautical miles, or **A3** of 640 miles. All give reaching or running courses with close fetches home. **A1** has a final short beat.

Port **B** offers shorter distances in coastal hops, **B1** with short daily beats and a long run home, total mileage 210 and **B2** gives a long run to begin with and short windward hops home, total 200 nautical miles.

Plainly, boats based at port **B** can also make longer cruises to the island or the distant shores but crew strength and time available, in that order, must be the deciding factors. Bad weather could hold a yacht weatherbound in port or force the gamble of a wild dash for home at the expiration of a holiday.

Cruising is pleasure and leisure. It should not be made a matter of time keeping and running to schedule – that belongs to life ashore.

91

Passage making preparations

A sound suitable cruiser, with the necessary stores for living, repairing and navigating must be assumed. **A.** Charts, pilot books, an almanac, tables, instruments and chart table equipment must be up to date and functional. The skipper should have mastered basic navigation.

The basic essentials are steering compass, log and hand lead or echosounder. These instruments are only as valuable as they are accurate and, if accurate, they are only as valuable as the skill of their user. A chart which has not been corrected up to date is a potential danger.

Likewise too few charts. Have large scale harbour or river charts also detailed coastal charts and save the small scale charts for open sea passage making.

Follow meteorological reports consecutively and begin listening to them two days prior to departure so that the weather trends can be appreciated.

Read all you can about the cruising area well in advance, so that pilotage information consulted en route is then familiar. Page mark vital information. Work out courses and distances, tidal streams and passage plans. In all likelihood these will have to be abandoned because conditions may make other plans necessary, but the problems will by then be familiar.

Accurate instruments

B. Make regular checks on compass and log. A simple check of steering compass is to take bearings on mast and backstay in line, from an inflatable (therefore non-magnetic) dinghy towed astern while motoring on a steady heading. Take each main heading in turn (N, NE, E etc) and note the difference between dinghy hand-bearing compass and ship's steering compass.

First check hand bearing compass ashore against known chart bearings. A bucket towed from the dinghy stern may be needed to hold her straight.

The log can be checked against that of a fellow yachtsman or whenever a 'current free' opportunity to run between fixed sea marks can be taken.

C. Some coasts have measured distances (x) shown on charts, used for checking ship's speed against log. Make timed runs at slack tide, or if there is a tidal current, take the average of several runs.

The weather

In some latitudes the weather follows predictable seasonal patterns, in others it varies continually. There are also the regions where summer calms prevail punctuated by violent winds peculiar to the climate and the area, such as the 'southerly buster' of the Antipodes or the Mistral of the western Mediterranean. The cruising man must know his climate and know what to expect.

In areas where high and low pressure systems follow in succession, fine weather and rough weather alternating the 'story' must be studied for a few days before sailing. In this way a skipper begins his cruise with a knowledge of the developing pattern and the subsequent weather forecasts make much more sense to him.

In the very simplified weather map shown here, the numbers represent a period of five days. In (1), depression **Y** is passing, with decreasing wind and clearing sky. By the next day, (2), a ridge of high pressure is approaching which continues into the following day, (3), with sunny seas and calm sailing. The unwary, who is not watching his weather could be tricked into embarking on a long passage but, days (4–5) see the arrival of depression **X** and a resumption of windy weather.

A wise skipper would realize that the improving weather was merely a pressure ridge between two lows. He would either advance his plans in order to make his passage while it lasted, or he would be prepared to hole up in shelter until the second low had gone through.

Not only wind strength and sea state will be affected but wind direction also and the shifting winds will be a major influence on his passage plans. In areas where summer calms prevail, he may have to make his sailing passages according to the onshore–offshore thermal winds of daytime and early night – or he fuels up in preparation for long passages under power.

Planning the legs

Long, hard beating to windward is to be avoided as much as possible when cruising, and a skipper plans his legs accordingly. He does so, however, knowing full well that his plans may have to be revised as he goes along. In some climates passage plans based upon expected wind direction are barely possible, winds varying constantly from calm to fresh breeze and boxing around the compass.

The chart shows a typical case of planning for a fairly reliable prevailing wind. The destination is the offshore island, but rather than making for it on a close-hauled leg, lasting perhaps 48 hours or more, the navigator–skipper works to windward along the coast in two hops of 45 and 75 miles to **B** and **C**, spending a night in port between them and another before tackling an easy reaching leg of 130 miles to the port **D**.

The rest of his cruise includes another short beat, **E**, a fetch back to the small island, **F**, and an easy run home (dotted course).

Tidal strategy

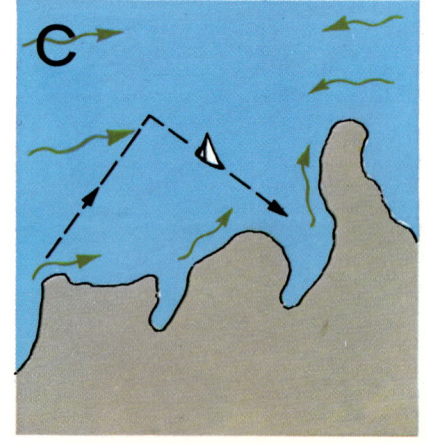

In waters beset by tidal streams a small sailing craft must 'work' her fair tides, particularly if her course lies to windward when she is coasting.

Our skipper has a leg of 45 miles to windward before him and he knows that he must use the full 6 hours (approximately) of fair tide to best advantage. Thus he may count upon (let's say) an 8-mile lift, leaving 37 miles to be made good.

At **A**, he drops down river the previous evening and anchors at the mouth, where he waits for the foul tide outside to ease. At **B**, he gets under way and with one hour of weak foul tide still to run he gets well to sea. This means that he will be in the best position to take full advantage of the tidal stream when it begins to run fair. With 37 miles to sail (two long tacks) he must average over 5 knots if he is to arrive before the tidal stream turns foul. If he cannot do this under sail, he may use engine power to maintain his average, or he may begin working closer inshore as soon as the foul stream sets in. Thus he may find slacker currents. He would of course need to be an efficient chart reader or to have local knowledge to do so in safety. At **C**, the arrows show how the tide is turning foul at the headland while still running fair close inshore.

In calm weather, an alternative is to kedge out the foul tide, lying to a kedge anchor for about 4 hours during the strongest period of the foul run. When kedging a tide, either at sea or in temporary shelter inshore, the ship is regarded as being still under way and a proper watch must be maintained.

D. On a longer passage offshore and across the run of the tidal streams, a series of foul and fair tides may be experienced. In our drawing, 3 floods and 3 ebbs are met with during the 36–38 hour passage. Starting from the bottom, the cruiser is carried downtide of her track (w) then back again (v) a number of times. The navigator has made an estimation of the time at which he might expect to make his arrival and at the end of 36 hours he hopes to be approaching land with the tide setting him nicely to windward (x) from a position downtide of destination.

It might happen that he is behind plan and (inset) at (y) well downtide of destination. He still has one windward-going tide to come but his arrival off the coast will be at a time when a leeward-going tide is about to begin, posing the possibility of being set downwind of destination. Accordingly he comes hard on the wind during the windward going tidal stream, to get upwind (z) of his track. He now knows that should the wind fall light or shift ahead as he nears the land, he has a commanding position from which to make his final leg.

97

Final approach

If the destination is unfamiliar and the passage has been long and tiring, extra care is needed in the final approach. Our cruising yacht may be at (a) or (b) and it is night. From (a) the loom of the town lights is visible over the hill, also two of the navigational lights. From (b) however a mass of town lights can be seen also. There may be a temptation to head straight for them.

The navigator must identify the navigational lights and then single out those which are the crucial ones for a safe approach. In this case a pair of leading or range lights must be brought into line from a position well outside the bay.

If pilot books and charts are studied in advance, the navigator will know what to look for. However, if anything puzzles him or doesn't seem quite right, the final run in must not be tackled until the mystery has been solved.

Harbour lights

Unless there are leading or range lights to provide a safe approach, careful identification of harbour entrance lights is needed, also a minute examination of the chart for any inconspicuous dangers – perhaps marked by an unlit buoy or beacon pole.

Quite often harbour entrance lights to small ports are fixed red and green. They may also be weak by comparison to other red and green lights in the town, such as garage, casino or advertising neon signs.

From well out to sea it is all too easy to head for the wrong light. Always approach from a fixed position thereby knowing what the *correct* light should bear from where you are. If you cannot fix your position accurately, proceed with extreme care, checking depth soundings against the chart. Decide from the chart where the dangers lie and shape your approach to avoid those areas until such time as you have sorted out the correct light.

Errors in pilotage

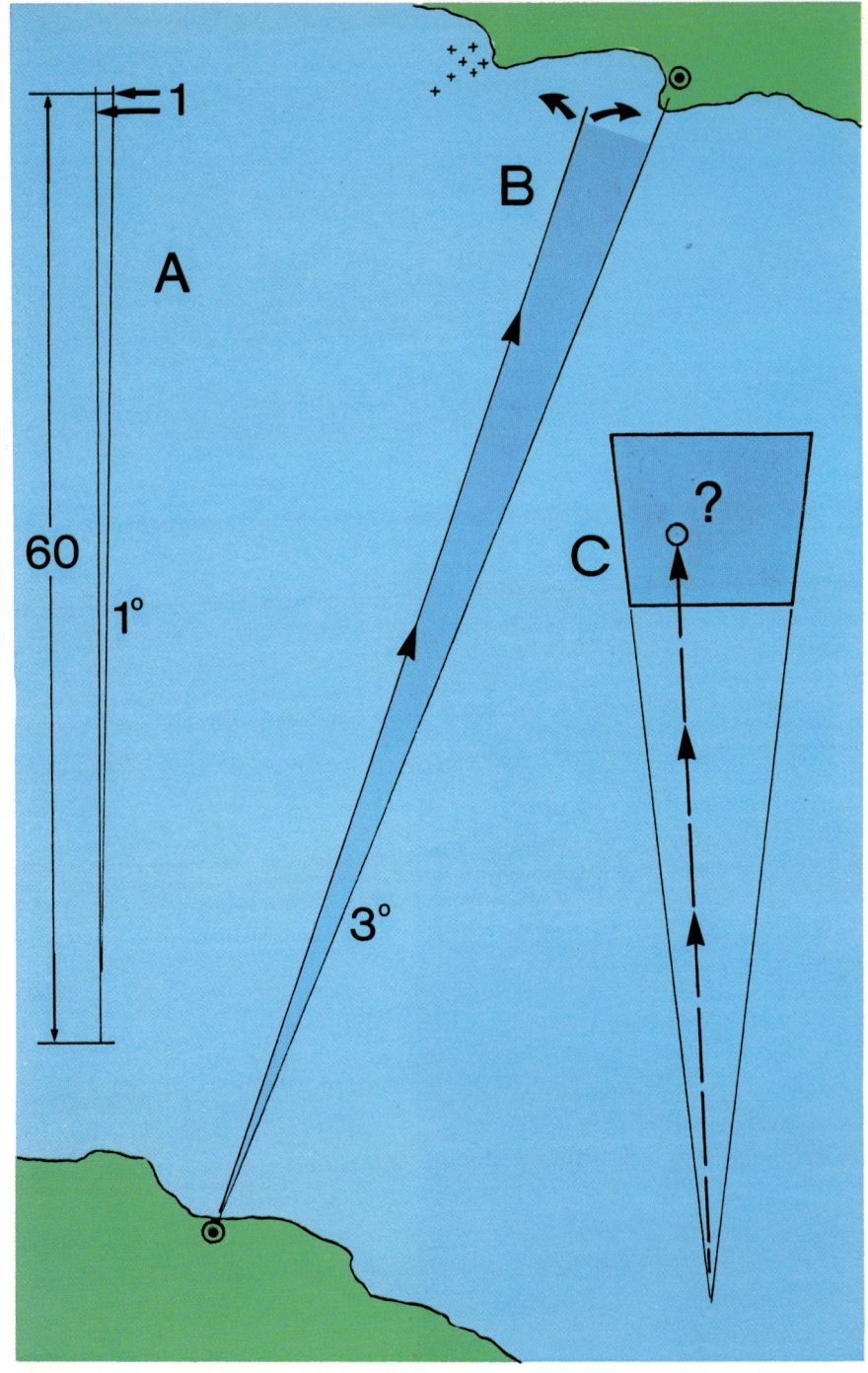

Basic pilotage, simple and safe, is essential knowledge for all seagoers but unsuspected errors can creep in which can be dangerous. By anticipating them, by recognizing them, they can be dealt with in time.

A steering or plotting error of only 1 degree represents a 1-mile off course error in a distance of 60 miles **A** and errors of 3 and more degrees are far more common. At **B** the port to port navigator sees two headlands when he makes his landfall. Not knowing his error, which should he head for? He might head confidently for where he supposed the port to lie, while heading for an unsafe stretch of coast. **C**. By making an appraisal of all possible errors to course (steering, compass error, tidal set, log error, leeway etc) he ends up with a 'box' within which his true position must lie **B**. Imprecise navigation perhaps, but he can now make a safer decision in his approach.

Drift and leeway

In rough weather the surface of the sea drifts to leeward but light displacement, shoal draft craft are affected by it far more than deeper, heavier boats with their lower immersion in more solid water. **D** will drift faster than **E**.

Side-slip while sailing or leeway also varies between boats and it varies too according to the angle of sailing and the state of the sea. Cruiser **F** is making 5 degrees of leeway in smooth conditions but at **G** with a rough sea meeting her starboard bow she may make a great deal more. A navigator must never assume that the leeway allowance made for one course will be suitable for all courses.

Leeway can be estimated by taking a bearing of the wake astern and checking it against the heading actually being steered.

Helmsman's error

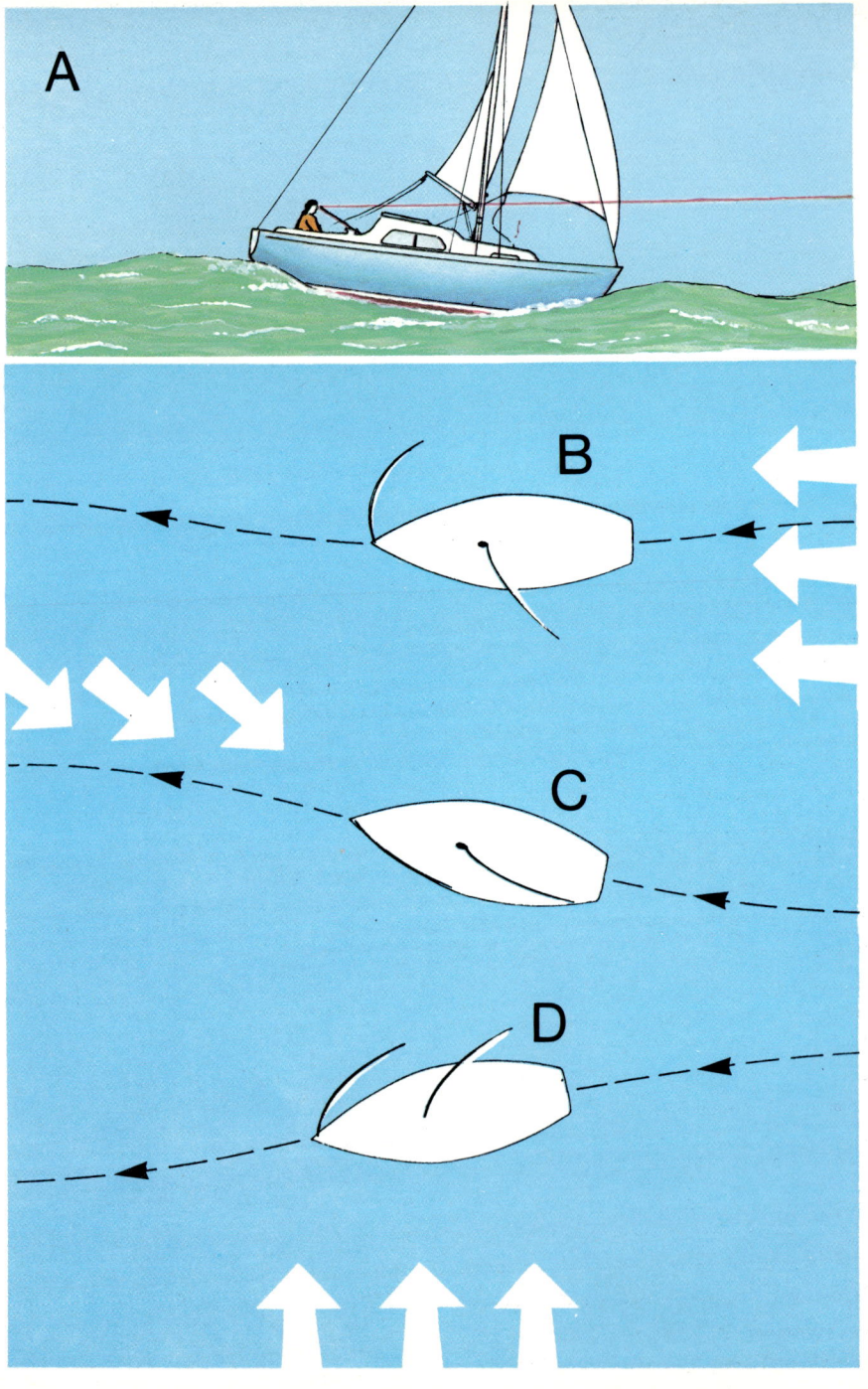

Concentration on steering compass alone tires a helmsman and can result in an erratic course made good. He should divide his gaze between compass, bows and horizon – the stars at night. This means that he subconsciously corrects the swing of the ship relative to the view ahead and, **A**, needs only an occasional glance at the compass as a check.

On the dead run **B**, a helmsman subconsciously plays safe to avoid gybe and tends to steer to windward. The use of a boom guy or vang to hold the boom forward results in more peace of mind and usually a better course steered. In rough conditions and an inexperienced man at the helm, it is better to order a course which he can steer, and keep to, rather than one he cannot hold. Closehauled, in a squally wind, the helmsman at **C** may have a tendency to luff, resulting in an error to windward. A broad reaching course in a cruiser **D** which carries heavy weather-helm will also produce an error to windward of the course plotted.

Log errors

E. A log over-reading of total distance run may be due to the steering of erratic courses by a series of poor or careless helmsmen. A log may under-read in drifting weather, when the cruiser is moving very slowly, **F**. This is often more noticeable in the case of a towed log rotator. **G**. Running in a steep, following sea may cause over-reading, but much depends upon the instrument and how efficiently it is installed. A towed rotator log suffers worst in these conditions, but other types, including electronic logs, are capable of over-reading. Ideally, any through-hull installation should feature two log impellers due to the constant variation in pressure, either side of the keel. Check at the start of each season. It is better to have a small *known* error than to assume accuracy.

Accurate knowledge of distance run, when approaching the coast in bad weather and low visibility is vital. Not always can radio bearings be relied upon or echo sounder readings be trusted to tally with the chart.

103

Anticipation

A long awaited light appearing suddenly, just where it should be, encourages the navigator to believe that he is sailing course **B** and seeing buoy (y). He may even see lights on shore which tally with the expected haven lights and he alters course towards them.

In fact, he was on course **A**, heading for buoy (x) and the 'haven' lights were pure coincidence. Unless he is very lucky he may be wrecked.

Always identify a light positively by its type and light characteristic first, even if you believe that it is the one you want. Then check the chart to find a corresponding description. Be especially vigilant when you are tired. Hallucination concerning lights at sea is a common pitfall for tired seamen.

Horizon errors

From eye level in a small cruiser the horizon may only be about 3.5 miles away. Thus, objects beyond this distance will be partly or wholly hidden from view. The buoy **C** 'dips' up into view and at night its light may be hidden intermittently by wave tops, causing a false light sequence to be seen. Check distant buoy sequences several times. The best aid is a stopwatch. Check beyond any doubt the time sequence and *then* consult the chart. This averts the risk of making the light fit the chart or wishful thinking. Note that the mountain peak **D** would be the only part of it visible by day.

At extreme range, a coast might appear as in **E**, the foreground hidden by the horizon. In poor visibility extending only to **X**, the same coast, **F**, looks quite different as it is the foreground cliffs which hide the high land beyond. Thus a coastal outline can vary between a series of sharp, distant peaks and a grey wall – even a sudden view of a line of surf!

False headlands

Headlands dominate most coastal passages: faster currents, rougher water and offlying rocks make many of them miniature Cape Horns. They can also deceive.

A. The cruiser, closing with the land at (1) may mistakenly think himself to be at (2) and in safe water, the coastal bulge looking from inshore like a headland. If he moves seaward to (2) however, the real headland comes into view beyond.

At **B**, **C** and **D** another headland has three different faces according to the position of the viewer. A navigator may have a preconceived idea of the appearance of a headland from an earlier visit. He may approach it a second time from a new angle and not recognize it – or mistake some other headland because it looks familiar.

Angles can deceive

E. The cruiser is leaving harbour. The navigator knows that the buoy outside the harbour, which he must make for, lies straight to seaward from the harbour entrance and so he fails to plot a course to steer.

He has been berthed in basin (a), therefore his course from basin towards the entrance is an oblique one, but he *feels* as if he were going straight out, as if from (b). He sees the nearer buoy, guarding the shoal, and makes for it, leaving it to port in the belief that it is the more distant fairway buoy. He runs aground. Always check by the compass heading. Never make casual assumptions.

False headings again

Pilotage by eye calls for a keen sense of direction, position and orientation. It is an art which is only slowly learned for some and a natural gift for others.

In the situation below there are three beacons, (a) on a distant shoal, (b) outside a submerged breakwater and (c) on the visible breakwater. The navigator sees the view at top left, but fails to take account of the distant beacon (a), assuming carelessly that (b) is the distant rock. He rounds the breakwater, crossing the dangerous submerged part – or attempting to do so.

Often, what appears to be obvious is actually a snare for the unwary. Close chart study and an ability to identify the features shown on the chart with the features seen and the angle of the ship's course relative to the lie of the land, are the secret of safe pilotage. When there are currents to contend with it can become risky to rely upon the eye alone.

The cruiser is being steered by eye on a course to leave the light-vessel close to starboard. No compass course has been set. In the diagram it can be seen that there is a strong tidal current setting on the port side and there are shoal waters to starboard. Being under engine in a calm, there is no wind direction to aid the helmsman's sense of direction. Although he maintains a heading that keeps the lightship on his starboard bow, the current is setting him fast to starboard, (a) then (b) then (c) and it is only a matter of time before the cruiser will be in shallow waters.

Sheering across a track can happen when heading almost directly into the current. The only safe means of discovering the error is to keep an eye on the steering compass heading.

False fixes

Compass bearings should only be taken on definite and identifiable objects, plainly shown on the chart. At **A** one bearing is reliable but the other, a headland, is not. Depending upon the state of the tidal height and visibility the extreme tip of the headland might appear as (1), (2) or (3). Whenever possible three suitably spaced objects should be chosen.

B The sighted objects chosen produce an angle that is too narrow to provide an accurate cross. The slightest compass inaccuracy or rough water could produce a wide area of error. Objects should be as near 90 degrees as possible and this angle be bisected by the bearing from a third object, if one can be found. In **C** the area of possible error is far smaller.

False soundings

D Layers of suspended silt or large shoals of fish can give a false echo-sounder reading. Errors due to use are more common such as the situation **E**. The yacht on her starboard tack encounters a more gently shelving river bed (1) as she approaches the bank than she does when on her port tack, where the steep-to bed results in an instant fall in echo-sounder reading. With so little warning she could run aground at (2). The following starboard tack takes her to (3), the 'sounder still showing deep water because she has run into a gully. When she tacks she will run aground.

In **F**, a landfall in fog, echo-sounder readings related to chart soundings could lead the navigator at (5) into thinking himself to be approaching the river at (4).

Deceptive chart scale

A. On a small scale chart a group of buoys may appear to be very close together, unless the scale is examined carefully. A navigator, rounding the bank which is guarded by three buoys might expect from a casual glance at his chart, to be able to see all three at the same time. In fact he might only see the nearest buoy, the others being mere pin pricks (lower view). Always try in advance to form a clear idea of what you can expect to see.

In buoy spotting it is also unwise to stare fixedly at where you *think* the buoy should be. Search the horizon systematically, even in directions where it might seem to be impossible to find a buoy. Course angle and minor pilotage errors play tricks on you and your buoy could be far to seaward where you'd least expect it.

Deceptive buoyage

B. This tacking yacht is unable to steer a direct course along the curving channel and this is confusing to her navigator's sense of direction. He should tack and put in a short leg (a) which permits him to tack again and sail up the channel. Instead, he sees the buoys aligned as in the lower view and stands on, ultimately cutting a corner into shallow water, (b).

The only safeguard when running a buoyed channel is to identify each and every buoy before approaching it and check it against the chart and against ship's *heading*. Unless a compass course is noted it is quite possible for a helmsman on the wind to luff for a wind shift and bring a (for example) port hand buoy over to his starboard bow – fooling the navigator who is conning by eye alone.

Coasting complications
– Apparent wind

True wind is that which is experienced while stationary, apparent wind is what happens to the true wind when a boat begins to move. At **A1** the 2-knot wind becomes an *apparent* calm when the running yacht is carried downwind on a 2-knot current. Conversely, **A2** if the 2-knot current was carrying her against the 2-knot wind and she was sailing closehauled at 2-knots, the total apparent wind felt would be, roughly, 6 knots.

At **B** a closehauled cruiser sailing at 6 knots, helped by a 4-knot current and facing a 24-knot wind experiences a gale force wind of 34 knots. Had she been running, with the current fair **C**, her crew would have felt only a moderate breeze of 14 knots. With strong currents and fresh breezes be prepared for very rough conditions when forces oppose.

Wind bend

Generally, the wind blowing along a coastline will 'bend' at the edge of the coast. (1), is the true wind and (2) is the wind bend crossing the coast. At (3) however, the wind is funnelling strongly down the valley, while at (4) there is an area of wind 'shadow' or calm under the lee of the cliff.

Where different air streams converge there may be eddies and a cruiser may encounter baffling shifts and violent squalls interspersed with short calms. Watch the water for signs of squalls but near high cliffs remember that they can strike downwards without such warnings. Watch other yachts, smoke, trees ashore and so on. Don't be caught unawares.

Coasting complications
– Headlands

If the headland is to windward, it will be necessary to have a fair current (in tidal waters) in order to round it by tacking. In fresh winds and strong currents the going will be tough.

Should the current be foul on arrival there are several alternatives. At nightfall and with a weary crew a return to shelter at **A** is wisest or you could stand out to sea into a weaker current **C** and smoother water. Anchoring temporarily at **B** until the current weakens is better than slogging it out without gaining much ground **D**. Then the crew can rest awhile and a new start can be made with the first of the fair current, which will be weak and the waters less rough than they will become when the current strengthens.

In non-tidal waters currents may also exist which remain constant in direction. Use of engine or standing well offshore to round the headland are alternatives which depend upon wind strength.

Thermal wind

In hot weather or in hot countries land heats more rapidly than sea, the hot air rising and the cool sea air flowing shorewards to replace it **E**. At night **F** the reverse happens and an offshore wind is felt. The effect may be felt up to 10–12 miles offshore.

However, if a 10-knot thermal onshore wind and a prevailing or a local pressure wind of 10-knots is also onshore, a strong 20-knot wind results during the day. Later, the reversal of the thermal flow after dark can result in a total calm (bottom). The presence of big fluffy cumulus clouds above the land is a thermal indication and the vagaries of inshore winds experienced may be due to this mixture of winds. The imbalance of temperatures ashore also gives rise to regional winds which can reach gale force with little warning.

Coasting complications
— Fishing craft

It is very important for a navigator to know and recognize the lights commonly carried by other vessels. He should also have ready at hand up-to-date information concerning less commonly met with lights such as vessels under tow, unusual vessels or manoeuvres and in particular the lights used by fishing craft, which when fishing have special rights of way. In different regions there are many types of fishing boat and only some common types are shown here.

The confusion of white and coloured lights which a cruising yacht may meet call for careful action and the fact that fishermen do not always display their lights accurately or clearly must be allowed for. It is not only the vessels which must be avoided however: lines and nets may extend far beyond a vessel and the direction of the gear is (or should be) indicated by the arrangement of her lights.

At (1), a drifter indicates the direction and distance of her nets by a lower white light. (2), pair-trawlers may indicate their gear by means of searchlights. (3), a ground trawler will be moving ahead or she may be stationary hauling her net. The pair trawlers, (2), showing green over white lights, are hauling their gear but the single trawler is under way and showing also her sidelights. Small crabbers, (4), work during daylight, using day signals (day signals also apply to all fishing craft and must be learned) and while shooting their long lines of connected pots they must be given absolute right of way.

Seeking shelter

Emergency shelter in bad weather and temporary shelter while waiting out a foul tide may need to be sought while cruising. Shelter from the wind however is not necessarily comfortable shelter or even safe. Waves bend as they pass along the land's edge, curving round and affecting open bays.

At (1), the island offers tenuous shelter for a short stay provided the yacht can lie close in shore and the bay, (2), may also remain quiet and clear of the wave pattern provided the wind does not shift and blow into it. The island, (3), however offers no shelter, neither does the shallow bay (5). The small enclosed bay, (4), is dangerous because a shift of wind could well trap the yacht sheltering there.

At **A** and **B** the two anchorages would offer shelter from the prevailing wind but should the wind change suddenly and blow onshore, **B** would prove to be a trap. Bay **A** on the other hand, would allow the yacht an easy escape on either port or starboard tack. Escape under sail should always be the objective for any vessel with sail as her main propulsion; the use of engine power is a bonus.

In seeking temporary anchorages note the weather trend existing and the local area forecast and barometer (if applicable to conditions in the area). Always keep the crew and vessel in a state of readiness for instant departure, plot a safe compass course for escape and maintain a running watch.

The coastal passage – Temporary anchorage

After anchoring select shore marks which are in line with each other or take careful compass bearings so that it can be detected if the anchor is dragging. With a change of current or a shift of wind, new marks and bearings should be found. If the yacht is swinging around or alternatively moving ahead and astern as her anchor chain rises and falls, the marks will tend to alter slightly.

Should she be caught in an open anchorage by a shift and an increase of wind, it may prove very difficult to recover the anchor unless a windlass is fitted. Usually the engine is used to motor up to the anchor but should the engine fail, the anchor will have to be *sailed* out.

This is done by making sail, suitably reefed, and laying off closehauled. The anchor cable will be dragged across the seabed until its increasing load prevents the yacht from going further. Before this happens she is tacked and her new tack will take her roughly in the direction of her anchor but this time she will be trailing slack cable over the seabed. The most experienced man aboard should be forward to haul in slack as fast as he can while watching the cable. The instant it begins to grow taut, indicating that the anchor is close ahead, he must take a rapid, safe turn around cleat or bitts. The jerk will be dangerously heavy in much wind but it will snatch the anchor out of the seabed. An inexperienced hand must *not* attempt this job unless the weather is moderate.

Coasting complications
– Haze

Coastal haze may be due to natural causes or to industrial air pollution and it may be quite local. In clear conditions the port **A** might be entered easily by lining up the church with the harbour beacon but in haze, **B**, the church has been lost to view, but a hilltop building might be mistakenly identified as the church spire.

A navigator's circle of visibility when approaching the coast, **C** is likely to be a narrow one and the view **D** could as easily apply to (1), (2) or (3). Try to estimate just how far you can see by dropping overboard a ball of newspaper and watching it disappear astern, but allow for possible variations in the density of the haze.

Current inset

In seas where tidal currents prevail then in hazy weather it is often possible to be set close inshore without realising it. This is due to strong local insets of the current at certain stages of the tide. At **E** the cruiser is on a safe course to pass outside the buoy, some miles away across the bay. At **F** a strong tidal inset is running and although the crew continue to steer their safe course, the cruiser has been set well *inside* it. In clear weather this fact would soon be noticed but haze prevents the use of shore bearing and other means such as radio direction finding cannot always be trusted so close to land, due to the bending of radio beams. Insets vary in strength and cannot easily be predicted.

Fog

Fog is caused by abrupt changes of temperature such as warm air coming into contact with cold water or land. Minute water droplets condense as in the case of a steaming kettle **A**. Poor visibility is one of the possible less pleasant characteristics of sailing towards an anti-cyclone.

Sometimes there is due warning of seafog, but not invariably. The arrival of a warm airstream in the advance of a suddenly deepening depression can bring fog. Usually fog is associated with calm weather and smooth seas – tempting to the passage-maker who gets well out to sea and then encounters dense fog, as he travels in an anti-cyclone, or area of high pressure.

Fog may be dense or patchy, shallow or deep, local or wide-spread, but common to all types is the distortion of sound, thus a ship's siren cannot be relied upon as an indication of distance away or of direction. Collision at sea becomes a great risk and yachts should try to get clear of main shipping routes and, if it is safe to do so, into shallow waters. Big ships will be intent upon avoiding each other and a small yacht can pass unnoticed.

At **B** local radiation fog may fill hollows, river valleys and low ground while remaining clear at sea. It usually disperses with the rising of the sun. The true sea fog, **C**, may be seen as a whitening of the horizon as the banks roll in. It may be extensive or there may be clear lanes between banks. At night, a yacht may be in clear air under a clear sky while all around her ship's sirens are sounding. The warm air stream in advance of a depression can mean both fog and strong winds, **D**, a very dangerous combination and one in which the radar signal returned by a small yacht labouring among big seas is likely to be small and uncertain.

127

Fog – The radar reflector

A radar signal is similar to a beam of light. It cannot bend around corners and a radar reflector with a surface placed at 90 degrees to the signal, like a mirror, will return the signal. (1), (2) and (3) show how a beam of light from a torch is either deflected (1), or returned (2). If a group of mirrors (3), all at 90 degrees to each other, is used the beam 'bounces' from one to another and then is returned. The familiar octahedral radar reflector is designed on this principle. No matter what angle it is to the radar signal, the signal will be reflected back.

This is why a metal mast will only return a good signal during the brief moments when it is at 90 degrees to the radar beam and a patchy 'blip' on the radar screen is the result. Don't rely upon your boat giving a steady echo in a seaway. Her gyrations plus the clutter of reflected wave crests may pass unnoticed. Moreover, the radar operator may not be paying full attention, or he may be using it at maximum range and miss an object close to. Sophisticated equipment expertly used may not miss you, but this cannot be taken for granted.

Horizon dip may hide the hull of a yacht. The ship using full range **A** may miss the yacht **C** which is inside the short range **B** and a deep wave trough may blanket a small vessel so frequently that any return signal she gives might be dismissed as floating debris.

Positioning the reflector

Every cruiser using waters frequented by big ships should have a permanently fitted radar reflector.
(1). The best position is at the masthead where it is at maximum height and not hidden by sails. (2). A minimum height above sea level of 10 feet must be sought or it will be below the horizon at long ranges. (3). A bow staff is a useful compromise, permitting an extra large reflector to be displayed in really dangerous situations. (4). Hoisted to the spreader a reflector bangs around unless it is also clipped to a stay.

The correct angle may be found by standing the reflector flat on deck. This is the 'catch-water' position.

Dry sails do not hinder a radar beam much, but when wet they may obscure a reflector completely.

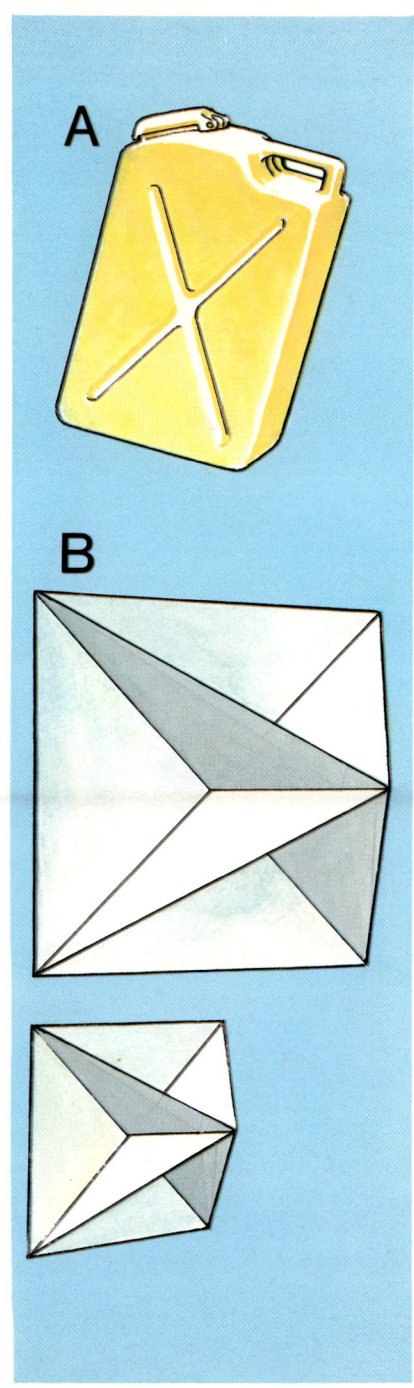

There is no substitute for a properly constructed reflector. The jerrycan **A** (also a foil-lined box and a square biscuit tin) were subjects for an experiment, but the returned signal from them was so intermittent that an observer would have discounted them.

B. The larger the reflector the better, the signal increasing by the square of the area. The argument that a small reflector of 1 ft corner to corner measurement is acceptable as half the value of a 2 ft one, and therefore suitable for a very small boat, is quite wrong – it would be many, many times less efficient. An 18 inch reflector is the minimum size for a permanent fitting. The angles of the plates must be exactly 90 degrees. Even errors of 3 degrees can cause a 50 per cent loss of efficiency. In dense fog the use of an umbrella-type folding reflector which has a fine metal mesh, opening to a 3 ft area is well worthwhile. On test, a reflector of this type gave a brilliant paint-up on the radar screen at 6 miles.

Fog tactics

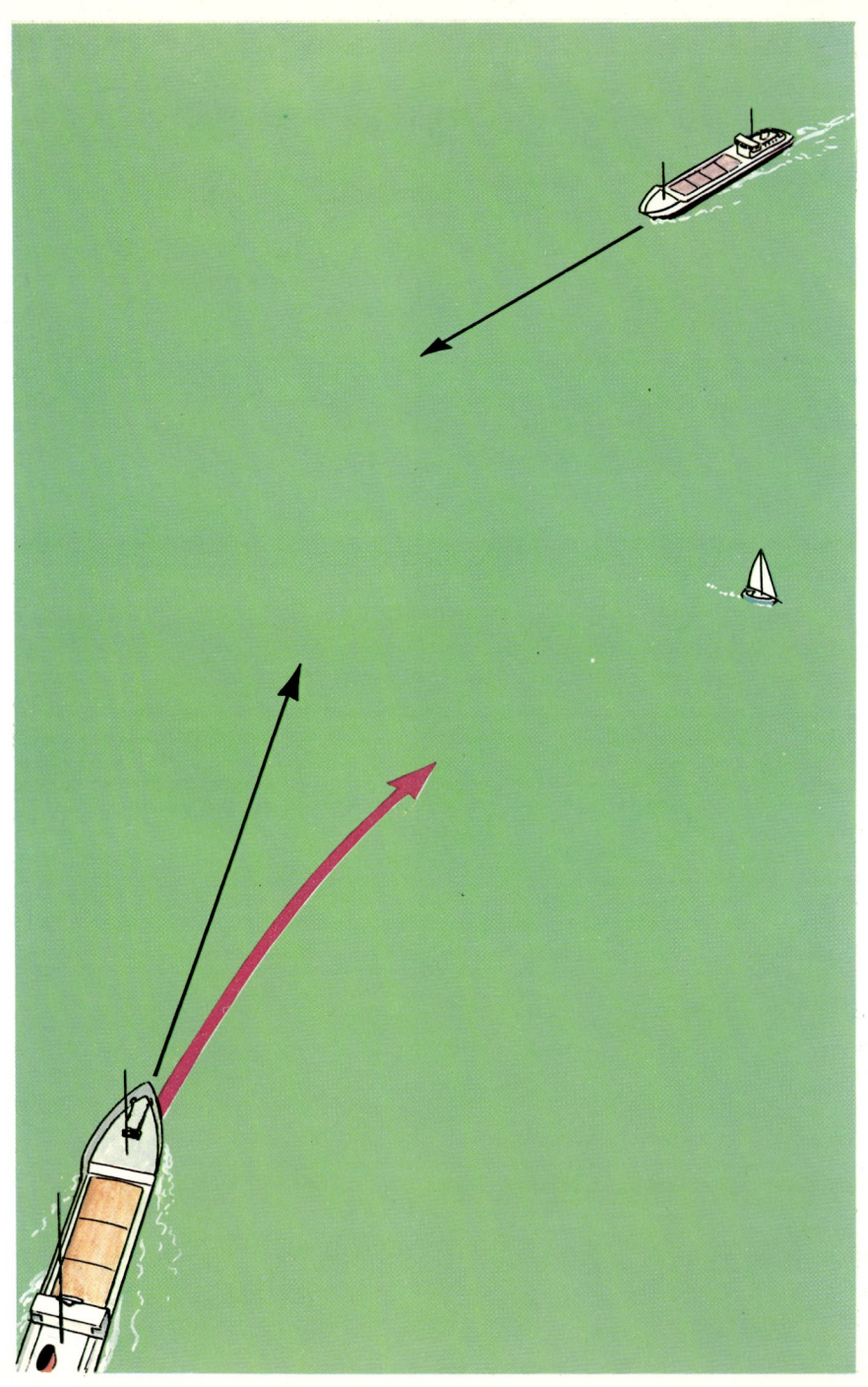

Avoid shipping lanes. If caught in one when fog descends, cross at right angles, show a radar reflector, sound your fog horn and maintain keen listening watch forward. Keep good steerage way on and all crew to wear lifejackets but not harnesses. If possible tow the dinghy. Don't suppose any ship's siren to be on your safe side because fog bends sound waves, muffles or amplifies them. *Any* other vessel is dangerous to you. Two big ships may be passing safely but then one, making an emergency evasive turn, may endanger you. If under engine you may have to throttle back at intervals in order to listen.

In very thick fog the reed of an aerosol type fog horn has a tendency to 'freeze' and lose power. Carry a mouth horn as well. Sound it evenly in all directions but not towards your crew or they will be temporarily deafened.

The aim should be to make for shallow water. Study the chart carefully in case your navigation is amiss and deep water extends close inshore to a rocky coast.

In fog, the first glimpse of a ship bearing down may be her white bow wave, or if the fog is thicker at sea level, her white bridge, although sometimes dark shapes show up first. You will have seconds in which to estimate her course angle relative to your own. Turning by bearing away may give you extra seconds.

You would not go to sea in a bad gale. Don't go to sea in foggy weather – it is far more dangerous.

Entering harbour

Some harbours have traffic signals to regulate incoming and outgoing shipping. These are listed in pilot books; read them in advance and await the entry signal, even if the entrance looks clear.

If entering foreign territorial waters, wear your own national ensign **A**, wear code flag Q (I request pratique and my ship is healthy), **C** and as a courtesy to the country you are visiting, wear a miniature of its maritime ensign at your starboard crosstrees **B**.

Listen for berthing instructions as you pass the harbour entrance hailing station. There may not be any, but obey them if there are because the Harbour Master has complete authority over the vessels in their movements within the harbour. Note and comply with any speed restriction signs.

When you know where you are to berth, consider wind direction and any current. Decide on your manner of approach and take your time. Give clear, concise orders to your crew and keep very calm, or they too will become excitable. Officials may be shouting and beckoning for you to hurry but they don't know your boat's limitations in stopping and you do. Don't attempt the impossible. You are the skipper. Obey any reasonable order but use your own judgement if it seems to be unreasonable.

In North America, traffic signals are rare, but in Europe particularly in harbours used by commerce, or where there are tidal basins, look for them.

Prepare your yacht

Be ready for all berthing eventualities.

D. Anchor unlashed and ready but stowed inboard.
E. A warp coiled ready for use on the foredeck.
F. Crew with a heaving line, sitting down ready on foredeck.
G. The boathook unlashed.
H. Spare fenders hitched to rail with slip knots.
J. Two fenders either side ready to drop outboard.
K. Deck crew sitting down to keep the view clear.
L. Spare crew standing ready but out of the way.
M. A warp coiled ready for use on after deck.

If the engine is unreliable, the mainsail can be stowed but ready for instant hoisting and a headsail can also be lowered but ready. If the dinghy is towing astern, the painter should be shortened up to avoid risk of fouling the propeller, should you have to go astern.

135

Bad weather

The new-comer to sailboat cruising should try to avoid bad weather until such time as he is competent to handle and navigate his boat in those conditions. He would be wise to gain his bad weather experience, if he can, by sailing as crew in a well handled boat, under an experienced skipper. It isn't always possible to avoid bad weather but you can read and think about it and you can make sure that your boat is equipped for it.

A calm sea poses few problems. The wind is the culprit and the sea is obedient to it. Study the wind and you have the secrets of the waves.

Strong winds and rough water are the ultimate test of man and boat. Any weakness in either promotes further strain and searches out new weaknesses. Violent motion, noise and fatigue make even simple jobs complicated and simple navigation difficult. Seasickness may impose even more strain. Learn your job so thoroughly in fine weather that the habit and instinct for doing things right will become second nature to you.

A boat with reliable engine, gear and sails needs a minimum of attention in bad weather. Proper stowage below prevents chaos and a good chart table with a safe stowage for books and instruments makes navigation far easier for a tired man. Ship-to-shore radio and an awareness that advice and help if needed are readily available, eases mental strain and reduces worry.

A Force 5–6 wind (17–27 knots) can produce a sea which can reduce crew strength seriously and it doesn't take a gale to cause trouble. The 34–40 knots of gale force is nearly double the force of a fresh to strong breeze but many beginners *think* that they have been out in gale force simply because a gale was forecast for their area at that time.

A Force 8 gale is a solid blast of wind and water and it can quickly develop into Storm Force 9–10 which is almost half as strong again. Small yachts can and regularly do survive, provided their crews keep their heads. A good boat and gear, open water and searoom to leeward are the essentials. Read all accounts of how other people fared, what they did and the mistakes they made. Don't make a panic dash for unsuitable shelter. Usually it is the crew that wrecks the boat – not the boat that fails her crew. Accept the fact that in a small sailing cruiser, crew strength will be reduced to one or two people by bad weather and plan accordingly. Be optimistic, keep up morale and don't give up.

Bad weather dangers

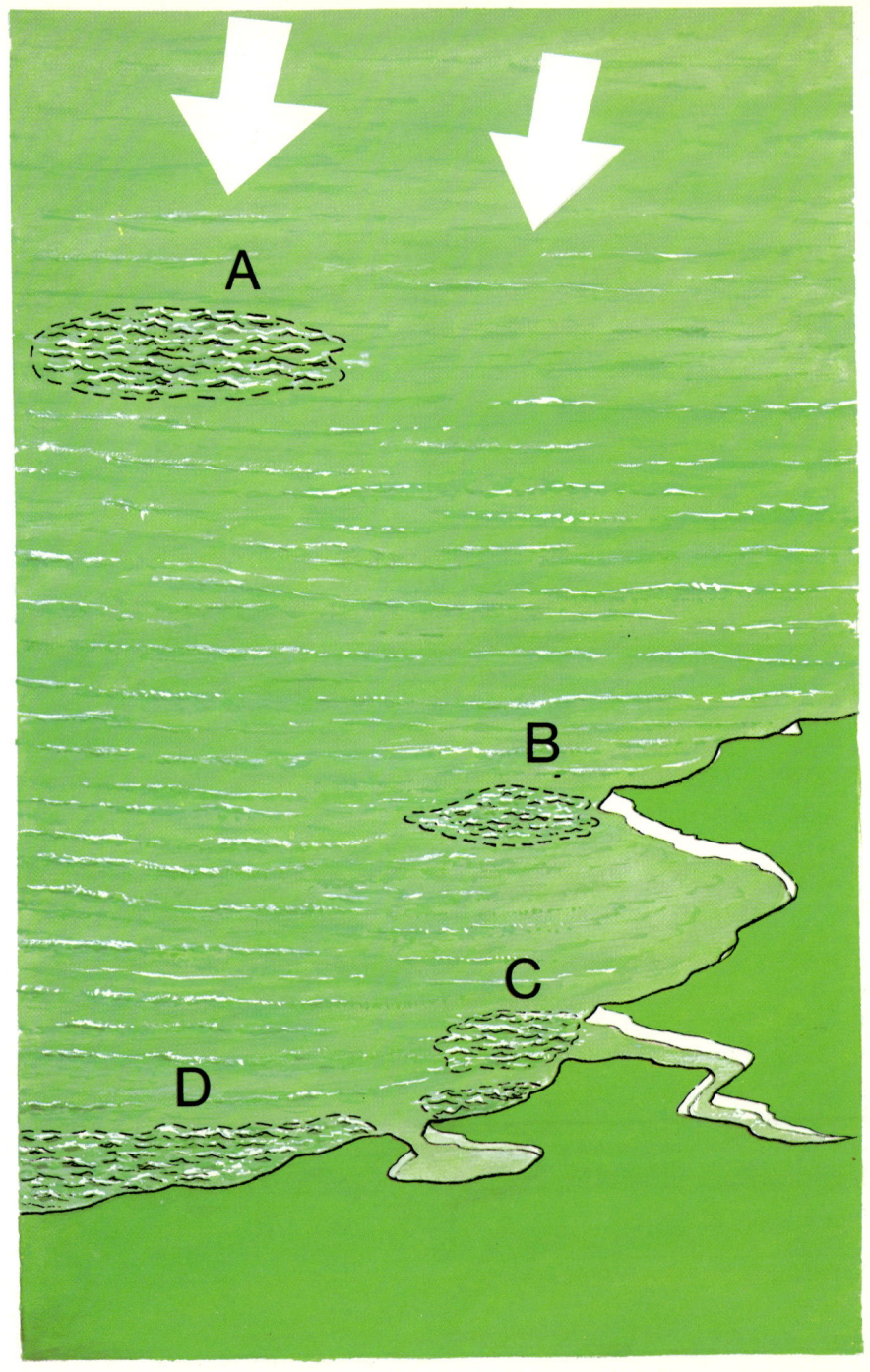

The waves and the land are the threats. Big ocean waves are not usually dangerous to small craft unless the cross sea of a wind change or some other phenomenon causes a big wave to rear and to break heavily aboard. Closer to land however a shallowing of the seabed **A** or strong currents off headlands **B** cause big seas to become shorter and steeper, liable to break.

Shallow water and/or an ebb current at a river mouth can render it dangerous to enter in bad weather **C** and a lee shore haven **D** which is difficult to find can be suicidal when visibility has closed down to a few hundreds of yards – the slightest navigational error can then be fatal.

Making for shelter

A low pressure system can travel forward at 20–25 knots, which means that if it is 200 miles away (for example) only about 8 hours remain in which to make shelter. During this time winds may rise rapidly to gale force and visibility may decrease. A small cruiser at sea may be run for shelter or she may be taken further seaward to gain a safer offing. This is the choice.

If we assumed that the boats at **E**, **F**, **G**, **H**, **J**, **K**, and **L** can all make 5 knots, boats **E**, **F** and **G** might make for the sheltering land to windward. **E** and **F** might manage it. Boat **H** is trying to get a safer offing to seaward but boat **J** is undecided. She is 40 miles from shelter but like **K** and **L** (20 and 30 miles from it), she might not get there before visibility closes down. The wise decision might be for **J** to make to seaward.

Winds can and do shift direction during a gale. This must be considered and contingency plans made.

Land and sea

The duration of a gale greatly depends upon local weather patterns. It may be a few hours brought about by the excessive sea breeze in a hot climate, or even several days when consequent upon other factors. A chain of depressions may cause a succession of gales interspersed by wind shifts and lulls.

A. Drifting at 3 knots, boat (x) has about 24 hours and boat (y) has 48 hours before the lee shore threatens them. When the duration of a gale is unknown, every mile of searoom is vital.

Waves can overwhelm a boat. The rogue wave **B** is a possible open sea danger, but a lesser one than the tide rip with its dangerous confusion of pyramidal waves. Poor visibility **C** poses great risk to a boat close inshore and making for shelter.

Big waves, otherwise harmless, can become a danger if a boat is run before them too long or too fast **D1** and **2** and her wake causes them to break. She may slew across them beam-on and be rolled over or she may bury her bow deeply and turn stern-over-bow. Damage is certain and very possible the loss overboard of crew.

Strength and good design are essential in the following:
(1) Reefing gear.
(2) Cockpit and rate of drainage.
(3) Companionway door or closure.
(4) Mast and rigging.
(5) Size and strength of windows.
(6) Efficiency of ventilators.
(7) Strength and security of fore-hatch.
(8) Height and strength of life-lines and pulpits.

141

Flooding

Hull openings, hatches and so on can let in great volumes of solid water unless strongly protected. Hatch boards should not be able to slide away or knock down and **A** shows a typically weak arrangement which could push inwards. **B**, with a full moulded recess, is better.

Plastic windows **C** can bulge under pressure and if set in a rubber strip they can flip out altogether. An emergency plywood shutter is a standby in case of trouble.

Many forehatches are secured only by a small bolt and violent pounding can loosen them, allowing them to blow open. A bad weather 'strongback' with a screwed hook engaging in an eye beneath the hatch is a wise precaution, **D**.

Cockpit

Very few cockpits drain fast enough to rid them of water if swamped, before successive waves arrive. **E**, if the companionway is open, much will pour below and although much water will be rolled out by the boat's motion, **F** she may remain sluggish and slow to lift her stern to other oncoming waves.

Keep the companionway boards shipped, have a properly fitted bilge pump and have a bucket stowed handy to the cockpit – it is probably the quickest means of emptying a cockpit.

G. If much water has gone below it will be difficult to pump out if the boat is pitching and rolling. It may be safer to turn head to sea and lie hove to while it is done.

Action

Boats, seas and conditions vary so much that one can only generalize about action to take. Getting an offing is a prime requirement if shelter is not possible.

A. Early, efficient reefing and use of engine to get well clear of lee shores in *good time* may be vital.

B. In a moderate gale situation, heaving-to may suffice, using a properly cut trisail and storm jib for preference. Hove to, a yacht may ride with some comfort until weather moderates. If it worsens and heavy seas begin breaking aboard other action is needed.

C. Running under bare poles is safe until boat speed reaches near-wave speed, when risk of broaching beam on or being filled from astern exists. The boat must be slowed down before this happens.

D. The accepted action in these conditions is to stream a warp in a large loop or bight. It must be of at least 300 feet length – longer if possible. The drag both causes crests to break well astern and slows forward speed to a safe limit.

In very extreme conditions running with a warp may become dangerous due to risk of a boat being pitchpoled forward or overwhelmed by a crest. A sea anchor (**E**) may offer safety although most modern hulls lying to one from the bow tend to lie beam on.

F. Drifting a'hull, helm lashed amidships and all openings battened down is an extreme measure dependent for safety upon the strength of decks and coachroof etc. Searoom is needed as a boat may drift at a rate of 2–4 knots.

Emergency equipment

Certain emergency equipment for seagoing yachts is recommended in some countries and required by law in others. The list varies a little but common to all are the essential basics:

(1) Two 3-lb fire extinguishers, regularly tested by manufacturers.
(2) At least two lifebuoys (see section on man overboard for other essentials).
(3) A powerful torch.
(4) First aid kit.
(5) At least 12 assorted distress signals.
(6) Daylight smoke signals.
(7) Lifejackets for all crew to national or official specifications (e.g. British Standard 3595 or US Coastguard PFD – Personal Flotation Device).
(8) Safety harnesses for all crew.

(9) Engine spanners and other tools.
(10) Navigational lights to official requirements.
(11) Spare fuel in reserve.
(12) Radio Receiver, and perhaps VHF radio telephone.
(13) Automatic liferaft or, at least, an inflatable dinghy.
(14) Powerful wire cutters.
(15) Adequate charts corrected up to date.
(16) Good binoculars suitable for night use.
(17) Reliable compass corrected for deviation

The crew must know where all equipment is stowed and how to use it. Extinguishers, torch, safety harnesses, lifejackets, flares and first aid kit must be in plain view.

Fire extinguishers and distress signals cannot be tested and if allowed to become out of date, damp or damaged they will almost certainly fail. Extinguishers are very vulnerable, especially dry powder types. Neither will help if careless use of bottled gas or petrol creates danger of an explosion. Leakage of these is one of the main hazards of life afloat.

Sailing is fun. Proper safety aids and sensible precautions make it more so because the knowledge that a boat is safely sailed is reassuring to the family and friends who are the crew.

Rescue

Code flag V (I require assistance) is not a distress signal and it is used when a tow is needed, to borrow fuel etc. Arm waving as shown means help needed, maybe an emergency. Code flags NC (or flashed or sounded on a fog horn) are used in distress, also SOS. Code word MAYDAY is the radio telephone distress signal.

Use distress pyrotechnics wisely. Altitude rockets are wasted if there is low cloud. Hand flares used in inflatable craft can drop burning cinder which could damage the fabric. Use flares in twos. Hold to leeward and don't look at them. A watcher may half-see the first but he will be ready for the second and might otherwise have thought he'd imagined it. You may have to wait for hours – have you enough signals? A yellow day smoke signal is a valuable aid to a searching helicopter.

Helicopter rescue

The mast of a rolling, pitching yacht makes it dangerous to lower a man on board. If the wire becomes entangled or if it is made fast, it can crash the aircraft. If possible clear away the backstay and with all sails down, motor slowly head to wind. If none of this is possible, yacht crew in lifejackets must be prepared to jump overboard one at a time to be picked up.

Better is to stream the dinghy downwind on a long line. If an injured crew member is to be flown off, send someone with him. If he has been given drugs or a tourniquet applied, send a message with him giving details and time at which the tourniquet was applied. Do as instructed: the helicopter crew are specialists.

Yachts and shipping

The International Rules for the Prevention of Collision at Sea must be obeyed but the increasing size of ships makes their ability to take quick avoiding action very difficult. In trying to avoid each other, the yachtsman may be caught in the middle. He must do more than obey the Rules, he must think far ahead because, despite his quick manoeuvrability, his is the slowest vessel at sea.

The illustration shows a dredged deep water channel in the approaches to a busy port, where big ships have an undisputable Right of Way over yachts and small craft. Crossing such a channel calls for judgement of the speed and manoeuvrability of the big ships.

Yacht **A**, planning to cross between ships, (w) and (x) will be too close to the bows of (w) and in danger from the approaching (y).

Yacht **B** is crossing obliquely and she will be longer at risk than yacht **C** which is crossing more at right angles and using her engine to get across quickly ahead of ship (z) and well ahead of ship (x).

Yacht **D** bears away under the stern of ship (z) but by mid channel ship (x) will be bearing down on her fast. She must then either gamble on getting across, turn back, or head down the centre of the channel, which may worry the pilot of the ship (x).

The angles of the masts of approaching ships is the yachtsman's guide to their heading but a bend in the channel can be confusing. The yacht **D** has the masts of ship (x) in line and seems to be crossing her safely but by the time she has crossed astern of ship (z), the ship (x) will have altered her course on the bend and she will be on a collision course with the yacht.

Situation **E** shows a yacht in the proximity of two small coasters. The coaster at (1) will have to give way to the coaster at (2). She blows one blast signifying a turn to starboard. The yacht is now at risk unless she too turns to starboard.

Small commercial craft don't always give way to sail. At sea they may be on autopilot with nobody on the lookout for quite long periods. They may also be on radar watch only (big ships also). Make allowances for human error on the bridge and stay clear.

The open sea

Big ships cannot stop or alter course quickly. At **A** the ship may take 2–3 miles to stop, even with engines full astern. At **B** the ship is turning hard a'port with her stern swinging far out of line so that while her bows might miss a small vessel, her stern could hit it.

The ship at **C** is making a wide turn on to a new course. The yacht at **D** sees her come bows-on and motors fast to get clear but the ship has not yet settled on her new heading and she is yawing. By the time she is steady **C**2, a collision situation is building up.

In sketch **E** the red yacht has the ship on a bearing which doesn't alter as the vessels converge – evidence of a collision situation. The green yacht finds that the bearing changes steadily as the two vessels draw nearer, showing that no collision risk exists provided both hold course and speed. At **F** a yacht makes a bold course alteration to avoid a ship, making her intentions plain. Small, erratic course changes can confuse the other vessel.

At **G** ship (y) is in clear view from the yacht and seems to be passing safely but the ship's radar shows ship (x) to be on a converging course with Right of Way. From the deck of the yacht, ship (x) may be hull-down over the horizon. When ship (y) alters course the yachtsman, not knowing why she has done so, may react wrongly. Be prepared for seemingly inexplicable behaviour.

153

At night

A. Never get close under the bows of big ships, day or night unless quite sure that they are moored or at anchor, there is a blind arc forward of the bows when viewed from the bridge. Remember also that while a ship's lights are plainly seen by the yachtsman, his own lights, when viewed from high on the bridge, may be lost against and among the waves.

B. If your bows are toward an approaching ship, steer a steady course, even when passing safely. From the bridge your navigation lights may otherwise show red and green alternately as you weave around. This could confuse a simple situation and lead to a dangerous course alteration by the big ship. (1), (2), and (3) show what the big ship sees.

C. Are your lights correctly aligned? Check them before making a night passage. This can be done in a marina by walking around and taking careful bearings of the light sectors.

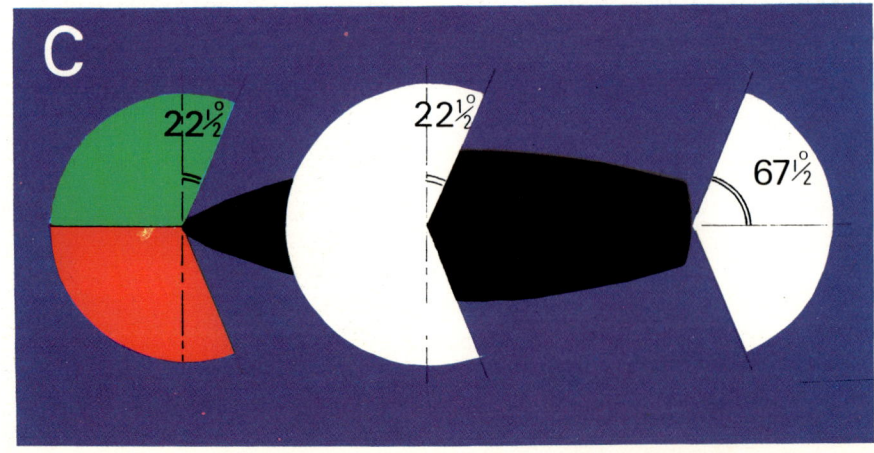

The big ship look-out may not see your lights. If in doubt it is better to switch on *all* lights, including spreader or crosstree lights, even though this may not comply with the requirements for a vessel under sail. BE SEEN.

There should be a powerful flashlight (not a toy), shine it towards the ship. Watchers will then see a sharp pinpoint of light whereas they might fail to see the diffused glow of a torchbeam shone upon your sail. Hold it steady. If you flash it on and off, watchers may assume that you are trying to send a Morse message. Remain alert until the ship is completely past – she could always make a last minute alteration of course.

The tender

Most cruising yacht tenders today are of inflatable type although our sketch also shows two rigid tenders of plywood or glassfibre construction.

The essentials are that a tender should be light, self-buoyant, of sufficient capacity to carry at least three adults safely in rough water. It should be robust enough to stand up to constant use and easy to row.

Although many owners prefer to use a light outboard motor instead of a pair of oars, these should be carried for emergency use; or at least there should be a paddle. Few inflatables row easily and in a fresh breeze with a full load aboard, it is all too easy to be carried helplessly downwind. When used at night the tender should have a torch aboard for use in case of pending collision or for signalling. Lifejackets should be worn and, ideally there should be a light anchor and line attached to the tender; a bailer of some kind is essential.

Records show an alarmingly high number of fatal accidents involving tenders, especially used at night. Overloading is a prime cause. There is a great temptation to embark from the shore, having managed to pack the whole crew aboard, leaving very little freeboard. Often that which is smooth close to shore, becomes choppy out in the tideway and it is then highly dangerous to either go on or to go back. Better not to start out overloaded.

At **A** an overloaded tender is being rowed with some difficulty by a man in the bows – the narrower hull at that point reducing his leverage on the oars. The stern is so low in the water that even a small wave can lop aboard. The trim of the boat is also wrong and this will make rowing even harder since the stern will drag and the rower will be pitched up and down, causing him to miss strokes. At **B** the tender is correctly loaded for her size, she is also properly trimmed fore-and-aft, with the rower seated at the most advantageous position.

A good (hard) tender may look like this (lower picture). Notice the buoyancy tanks permanently fixed below the thwarts or seats, the sensible fender around the gunwale and the provision for two rowing positions. With only two people aboard, the rower will need to sit at the forward position in order to trim the tender correctly.

Dinghy handling

If the cruiser is moored in a strong current, plan to arrive well forward to allow for seconds spent shipping oars before grabbing for the yacht's rail. Secure the tender's painter right away.

Other approaches may be by rowing crab-wise across the current or by dropping down-current towards the moored yacht, allowing the tender to pivot bows to the current while still above the yacht. By rowing to stem the current, the tender can be allowed to sidle in towards the bows of the yacht.

There are fewer problems to using an outboard motor, but an approach while stemming the current is always important. Steer straight alongside at a slight angle, cutting the motor when it is apparent that you are going to carry enough way to get there. Remember a stopped propeller has a dragging effect.

Be strict about the way in which passengers leave the tender. Keep her trimmed and ensure that the first man out takes the painter and holds the tender bows-in while others disembark.

It is unwise to tow any dinghy in a rough sea, especially a following sea, when a hard tender will run up on a wave surge and crash into the parent boat's stern. In more than a moderate breeze an inflatable is liable to flip over. Tow it on a very short scope and first remove all loose gear. Better is to stow it on deck, half deflated and well lashed down.

Transferring crew from a dinghy towing alongside is risky. Weight in the bows will cause the tender to bore with her bows and to fill. Keep weight slightly aft of amidships and if transferring from cruiser to dinghy, sit down at once.

River bars and shallows

(1) Viewed from seaward a breaking bar may look harmless but when seen from the land (2), the true state of the breaking water can be appreciated. Lacking local knowledge or a local pilot don't attempt to run a bar if it appears to be breaking. The best time to take a bar is usually between half flood and high tide and the worst time is around half-ebb.

An auxiliary sail cruiser is perhaps the worst type of design for shallow water surf, lacking the speed to run in between crests and having a keel which could be vulnerable on the bar, when deep in a water trough. The risk of being rolled or pitchpoled is also greater.

Upon arrival off a bar, note whether there is a swell running in from seaward; a long swell may pass unnoticed at sea but in meeting shoal water it steepens and becomes faster moving. Wind driven onshore waves may not in themselves constitute a bar hazard but combined with a swell they may become so. Bars do not always break continuously. Sometimes, many minutes may go by between heavy breaking seas. For this reason an apparently quiet bar may be a killer in disguise. Stand off in deep water and watch for ten minutes or so. If any doubt, signal for a pilot or make for some safer haven.

Once the run in has been started there is no going back. The sight of a big, breaking sea astern is demoralizing, but to attempt to turn back into it is highly dangerous.

Crossing offlying shallows poses similar problems although there is usually less reason for so doing. If there is a deeper channel over the shallows, remember that it may have shifted and if it is not buoyed proceed slowly on echo-sounder, steering a serpentine course in order to feel out the lie of the shallower water on either side. The aim is to know in which direction you must head should you bump bottom. The presence of current can also show roughly how it lies, the water appearing smoother when wind and current combine, slightly rougher when they oppose.

161

Calculating depth

Before approaching a bar or a shoal you must know what depth of water you can expect to find at its shallowest part. Remember though, that strong prevailing winds and barometric pressure can alter the height of water in a tidal estuary.

A simple, safe method is to take several position fixes on the approach, noting depth found at each position against depth shown on the chart. In the drawing, a yacht is heading in on leading or range marks. A fix at **A** and a sounding shows 7 metres depth by echo-sounder and 5 metres on the chart. At **B** she finds 5 metres (chart 3 metres). Thus, with a difference to expect of 2 metres, the depth at **C** on the 1 metre shoal should be a total 3 metres.

In the diagram:
   D = Neap Tide
   E = Spring Tide
   F = Mean Tide Level
   G = Chart Datum

In rough terms, a tide will rise (or fall) its full range in 6 hours (actually a little more). One quarter of this movement in the first two hours and one quarter in the last two hours and the remaining half of the total movement during the middle third and fourth hours. Thus the level changes rapidly during the middle of the tide.

Note that Low Water Springs is considerably lower than Low Water Neaps.

First find the day's RANGE (height of the day's low water from the day's high water equals Range). Another method is to take Mean Level × 2 minus Rise for that day as approximate Range.

The height of low water can be found by subtracting Range from Rise. Depth at any state of tide will now be found approximately as follows:

Example: 2 hours ebb at Neaps will leave three quarters of Range, plus height of low water above Chart Datum, plus chart soundings below Chart Datum.

Remember, at half tide (Mean Tide Level) the depth is the same at Springs as it is at Neaps. At low water Neaps there will be more actual depth than there will be at low water Springs.

163

Eating and sleeping

Food and rest are essential to fitness and alertness at sea. Sophisticated cooking may be impossible, but a pressure cooker **A** is safe and simple for stews and many other dishes. **B** A galley cooker should swing in gimbals and the cook should wear oilskins as protection from boiling water spillage, and a harness strap can be used so that both hands are free. The waffle or sandwich toaster **C** simplifies making hot snacks.

Vacuum flasks **D** permit advance cooking of hot food prior to a passage, or they can be used to keep cold foods crisp and fresh. Avoid overloading 'fridge or icebox **E** with foods which could be carried in canned or dehydrated form and reserve it for salads, meats, milk and cold drinks in hot weather.

Choose mealtimes, not by the clock but when crew is free to relax and when it will not interrupt the sleep of the watch off duty. Don't serve up just when the ship is about to be worked through a difficult channel – ask the navigator whether any manoeuvres are imminent. To be of value, there must be time to digest a meal properly and calmly.

In weather too rough for cooking in safety, boiled eggs, chocolate, cheese, nuts, raisins, fruit and fruit juice offer all the nourishment needed. Drink plenty of liquid because dehydration, especially after seasickness, is a snare at sea.

Sleeping at sea

Lee cloths **A** are essential. Otherwise a sleeper feels insecure and cannot rest. Simple rectangles of canvas secured to the bunk base and triced up as shown will suffice.

At sea, an athlete's track suit **B** is ideal as it can be worn as it is, or under heavy clothing and on a night passage it can be slept in, leaving the wearer ready for a quick call out.

C. With a box berth, proper ventilation at the pillow end is essential otherwise the sleeper is breathing his own exhaled breath and he will awake thick headed and half doped. Holes drilled at face level are all that is needed.

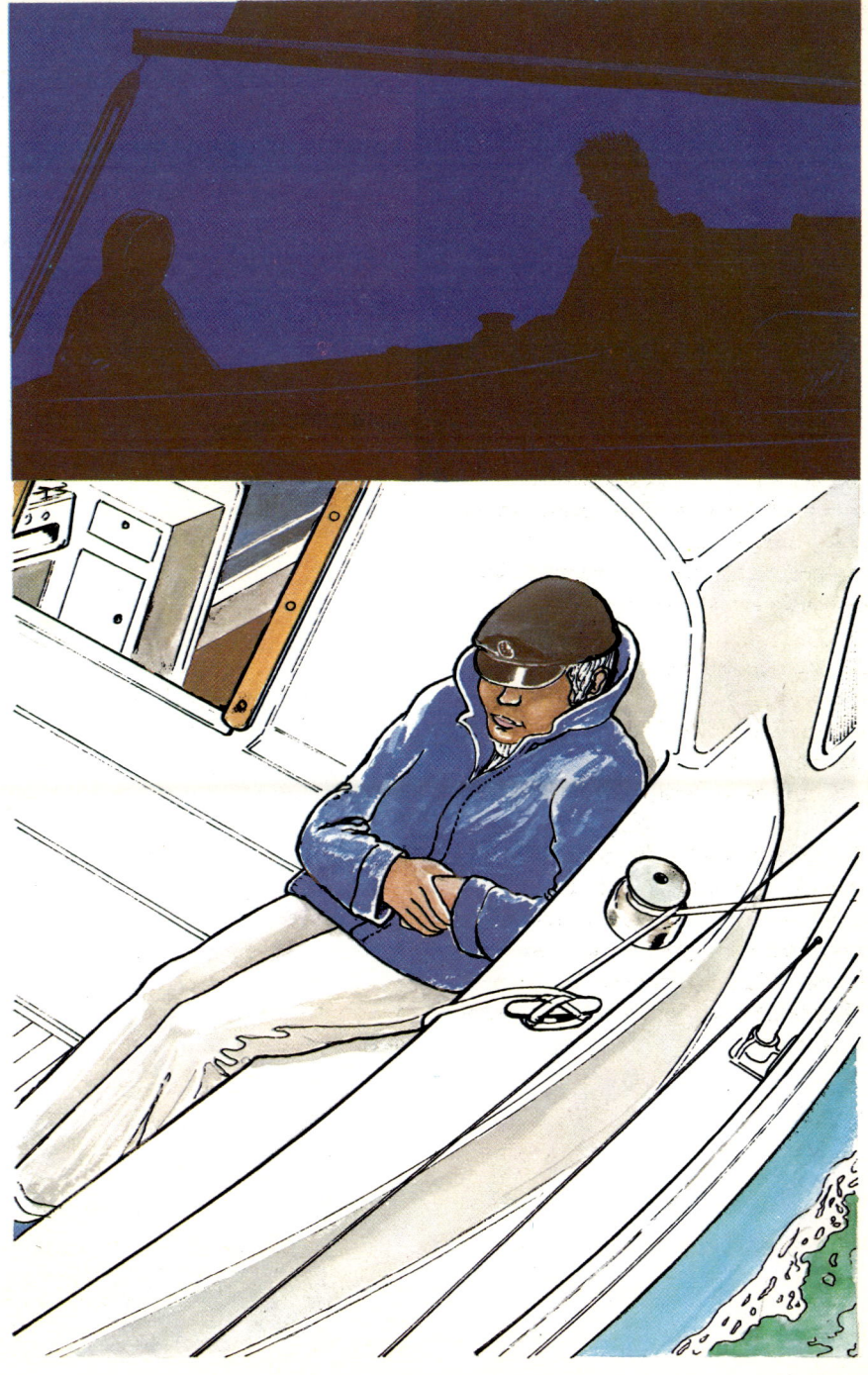

Never hand over the night watch to a newly awakened man. Give him time to become fully alert. During the early stages of a sea passage nobody feels that he has had all the sleep he needs and it may take a full ten minutes before a sleepy man is fully alert.

At the start of a passage don't panic if you cannot sleep, by your next watch below you will sleep soundly. When a person is really exhausted though, he must have sleep. At a pinch, a man cat-napping in a corner of the cockpit can keep going indefinitely. Watch out for the dozing helmsman though and see that he has his safety harness hooked on.

Rather than enter tricky waters with a crew of sleep-walkers, it is better to heave-to and rest, with one man at a time on look-out.

INDEX

Anchoring 12, 35, 60 et seq, 121, 122, 135
Balance 14
Ballast 18
Buoyage 113
Charts 92, 93, 98, 103, 112
Cleats 41, 84
Clothing 38
Cockpits 143
Crewing 86, 88, 135, 164
Cruise planning 90, 92, 95, 96, 97
Cruising preparations 38, 135
Dinghy 135, 156 et seq
Displacement 8
Distress signals 146 et seq
Drifting 8, 10, 101
Emergency Equipment 146
Fenders 135
Fishing craft 118
Flooding 142
Fog 124, 126 et seq
Fog Horn 133

Gybing 51
Handling, narrow waters 58, 59
Harbours 134
Headlands 106 et seq, 116
Heaving-to 13, 57
Heaving a line 85, 135
Heeling 14, 18, 24
Helicopters 149
Hull shape 8, 9, 14, 19, 20
Lee helm 11, 12, 17
Lee shore 22
Leeway 101
Life jackets 38
Man overboard 76 et seq
Marinas 31 et seq
Moorings 69
Night sailing 99, 104, 118, 154
Pilotage 100 et seq
Power 23, 38
Power handling 26 et seq, 37
Propellers 23, 25
Radar reflector 128 et seq

Reefing 16, 70 et seq, 123, 141, 144
Rescue 148
River Bars 160
Ropes 80 et seq
Safety on deck 44
Sail setting 42, 43, 46, 48
Sail changing 74
Sheets 40, 43, 50, 51
Shipping 132, 150 et seq
Sleeping at sea 166
Soundings 111
Strong winds 11, 17, 29, 35, 38, 102, 114, 120, 136, 140
Tacking 50
Tender 135, 156 et seq
Tides 96, 97, 125, 162
Watches 87, 167
Weather 94, 126, 136 et seq, 139
Weather helm 16
Wind behaviour 114, 115, 117
Wind shifts 22